D0540382

THE RUGBY REVOLUTION

THE
RUGBY
REVOLUTION

DEREK WYATT
& COLIN HERRIDGE

metro

Published by Metro Publishing Ltd,
3, Bramber Court, 2 Bramber Road,
London W14 9PB, England

First published in hardback in 2003

ISBN 1 84454 004 9

British Library Cataloguing-in-Publication Data:

A catalogue record for this book is available from the British Library.

Design by ENVY

Printed in Great Britain by CPD (Wales)

1 3 5 7 9 10 8 6 4 2

Papers used by Metro Publishing are natural, recyclable products made
from wood grown in sustainable forests. The manufacturing processes
conform to the environmental regulations of the country of origin.

Pictures reproduced by kind permission of Action Images.

Every attempt has been made to contact the relevant copyright-holders, but
some were unobtainable. We would be grateful if the appropriate people
could contact us.

'The Running Game' reproduced by kind permission of Peter Fenton.

To Jo, Daisy and Jack and
Sandy, Amanda and Justine

CONTENTS

ACKNOWLEDGEMENTS

Colin Herridge is largely responsible for this book; he approached Derek Wyatt back in the early part of 2001 to ask if he would help write a follow-up to his earlier book Rugby DisUnion. Derek agreed to come on board but wondered how, as a working MP, he would find the time

It is Colin who has done much of the work, particularly with the research. He ended up with 40 hours of taped interviews, with additional material from dozens of discussions with a whole range of people involved at various levels in rugby around the world. We are grateful to those listed below who consented to being interviewed and to many others who preferred to remain anonymous.

Our thanks go to: Brian Baister, Bill Bishop, Nick Chesworth, Bob Dwyer, Dennis Easby, Trevor East, Mark Evans, Ian Ferrier, Ian Frykberg, Tony Gadsby-Peet, Mark Gay, Roger Godfrey, John Hall, Tony Hallett, Phil Harry, Bruce Hayman, Mike James, John Jeavons-Fellows, Charles Jillings, Donald Kerr, Roger Looker, Roy Manock, John Mason, Dick McGruther, David Moffett, Brian Moore, John Mulford, John O'Driscoll, Simon Poidevin, Dean Richards, John Richardson, Budge Rogers, Ross Turnbull, Peter Wheeler and Vaughan Williams.

Thanks also to Chris Rhys and Adam Hathaway for help with the various statistics, and to the RFU Museum of Rugby at Twickenham.

Colin also had access to all-important minutes and documents as well as hundreds of press cuttings from the period. He cajoled Derek to keep an interest in between division bells at 2.00am in the Lobby of the House of Commons and his ever-expanding mailbag from his constituents.

The outcome is *Rugby Revolution* – the story of the international game since it went open in August 1995.

We would both like to thank Jon Davies, our editor, and Adam Parfitt, Editor-in-Chief at Blake Publishing.

We both lead itinerant lives and without our respective partners, Jo and Sandy, we would not have quite the fun we have had writing this book. They have indulged us and we know who we will spend the advance on!

Derek Wyatt and Colin Herridge

GLOSSARY

ACT	Australian Capital Territory, a State rugby union side
AGM	Annual General Meeting
ARL	Australian Rugby League
ARU	Australian Rugby Union
CPMA	Callan, Palmer & Morgan Associates
CSI	Communications Services International
EFDR	English First Division Rugby Ltd
ERCA	English Rugby Counties' Association
ERL	English Rugby Ltd
ERP	English Rugby Partnership
ESDR	English Second Division Rugby Ltd
FFR	Fédération Française de Rugby

FIR	Federazion Italiana Rugby
FIRA	Fédération de Rugby Internationale
IMG	International Marketing Group, founded by the late Mark McCormack
IRB (IB, IRFB)	International Rugby Football Board
IRPA	International Rugby Players' Association
NSWRFU	New South Wales Rugby Football Union
NZRFU	New Zealand Rugby Football Union
OFT	Office of Fair Trading
PPMF	Players' Promotions and Marketing Fund
PRA	Players' Rugby Association
QRU	Queensland Rugby Union
RFU	Rugby Football Union (England)
RWC	Rugby World Cup
SANZAR	South Africa, New Zealand and Australia Rugby
SARFU	South African Rugby Football Union
SGM	Special General Meeting
SRU	Scottish Rugby Football Union
TWI	TransWorld International
WRC	World Rugby Corporation
WRFU	Welsh Rugby Football Union

ABOUT THE AUTHORS

Colin Herridge has been involved with the game of rugby from the first week he turned up at grammar school. Being the smallest boy, he was put in the team at scrum-half on the first games day, and stayed in that position until playing his last game of rugby at the age of 47 in a Golden Oldies Tournament in New Zealand in 1987, just before the first Rugby World Cup.

In between, he played for his Old Boys' side, Nottingham University, English Universities and the UAU, Notts, Lincs and Derby, Surrey and Rosslyn Park. He was press-ganged on to the Surrey Committee in 1971 while still playing and, over the following 30 years, had various administrative positions with the county including Team Manager, Chairman of various committees and President in 1991/92, as well as being made a Life Member of the county.

He was persuaded by JRC Young (a brilliant wing for Harlequins, England and the British Lions in the late 1950s and early 1960s) to become Chairman of Selectors at Quins in 1979, before taking on the role of Honorary Secretary in 1981, a position he held for 14 years. He also had time to succeed Dudley Wood as a Surrey representative on the RFU committee in 1986 when Dudley became the RFU Secretary.

Colin became Liaison Officer for a number of visiting international sides to England, including the 1988 Australians. Then in 1991, he was asked to become Media Liaison Officer for the England team and continued in that role until 1996, travelling with England through two World Cups and two Grand Slams. Despite being a member of the official England party, Colin even paid his own fare to South Africa in 1994 when England made its first visit after the abandonment of apartheid. The RFU believed that any extra body would be an added expense.

He has been lucky enough to watch or play rugby in many parts of the world. He was Treasurer of the RFU for a year before retiring in 1997. He continues to watch rugby every Saturday at Harlequins, Esher or Cobham or several other local clubs wherever, in fact, there is a match being played.

Colin is, and always will be, a believer in the amateur culture but understood and supported the move to professionalism. He had unique, first-hand experience of being on the RFU committee and seeing all the money coming into the game and also being with the team during the first half of the 1990s when players had to turn up on a dark, miserable winter's evening at Marlow in Buckinghamshire to train. The earliest most of them left was 10.00pm after grabbing a bite to eat. Then they would disperse to all parts of the country, some not getting home until midnight and then getting up early the next morning for work with club training on the Tuesday evening for good measure.

When England started to meet on the Wednesday before a Saturday International, some of the players had to take unpaid leave or just could not earn money while they were on England duty. It was hard to reconcile the hardships of Dooley and Richards (policemen) and Leonard (a carpenter) with the millions coming into the game via sponsorship, TV and gate receipts.

Colin also saw the state of the game in other countries, particularly South Africa, where no one bothered to disguise the fact that the players were being rewarded for playing in a variety of ways. In New Zealand, senior internationals were blatantly advertising on television against all IRB regulations.

The England players became more and more cynical about what was happening and this developed into outright hostility towards the governing body. When the announcement was made in Paris, Colin was surprised because, although he had heard lots of rumours in South Africa during the World Cup about what was supposedly being offered to players to join a rebel circus, he could not see the IRB going for a full hand.

*   *   *

For Derek Wyatt, playing rugby turned on passing the 11-plus in 1961. He had wanted to go to Southend High School because they played soccer, but Derek's father insisted he went to Westcliff CHS believing he would receive a better education. The trouble was, they played rugby.

He began as a second row because he was tall but, after scoring a number of tries, he was moved to the wing and, apart from the odd performance at full-back, centre or fly-half, it was on the wing that he stayed.

The Wyatt family moved to Colchester with Derek attending RGS there, and was captain in 1967, in which the team won ten and lost two. The following Easter, Derek played in an England trial at Oxford, despite a battle with asthma throughout his teens and early twenties.

Derek took a Teaching Certificate in History at St Luke's College, Exeter, where there was, at that time, a much better standard of rugby than Cambridge or Oxford, and there was fierce competition on the wing. Graham Angell played for three years on one wing, and Peter Knight three years on the other. Whilst there, Graham had a succession of England trials and Peter, ultimately, went on to play for England. So, Derek never quite made it at St Luke's, though the tries still came – eight on his début for the Freshers XV and four on his début against Weston-super-Mare for the First Team.

In his final year, Derek gave up rugby altogether as he was President of the Students' Union, his first taste of local student politics, where the President of the National Union of Students was someone called Jack Straw, now Secretary of State at the Foreign Office.

Before joining Bedford in 1973, Derek played one season with Chichester RFC and one with Ipswich RUFC. He loved playing for both clubs, and learned a great deal. At Chichester, it took an aeon to go from their Sixth XV to their First XV, but the wait was helped by the captain, Clive Phillips, a wise counsellor and still a good friend.

At Ipswich in 1972/73, the team reached the last 32 of the John Player Cup (then the RFU's knock-out Cup). Ipswich then was a formidable club, with several players like Phil Hardiman and Ian Hepton having had first-class experience at Wasps and trials for England.

At Ipswich, Derek scored over 70 tries and kicked the odd goal, so he felt he would benefit from moving on. But where next? His nearest club, Saracens, failed initially to respond to his letter, and when they did they called him 'David' and wouldn't pay any expenses. So Derek wondered if Bedford, a mere 80 miles away, would be interested.

Having dialled the number for Bedford, the man who answered was Budge Rogers, then holder of the most caps for England and a previous captain of England. He told Derek that they had six county wingers in their three teams including Billy Steele, the Scottish winger, who was just coming off a Lions tour. He promised Derek 20 minutes in the Bedford trial that weekend.

Having survived the trial, Derek was then invited to the next weekend's 'away days'. After arriving too early, he was eventually joined by back-row forward and former captain at Bedford, Tod Slaughter. He asked who Derek was. He then said, 'If I was you, I'd go back to Ipswich ... we've far too many wing three-quarters here.'

Derek stayed, and was then selected for the Second Team (better than anticipated) and struggled in his first game away to Leicester Extra 1st XV to make the grade. He then scored 18 tries in the next five games and was duly promoted to the First XV.

In his first season, Derek broke the Bedford record held by Alan Towersey, scoring 33 tries. Eventually, he scored 145 tries in 152 games for Bedford over the next five years, breaking his own record with 36 in 1975/76.

In between, Derek played in a County Final against Gloucestershire for Eastern Counties (finishing as runners-up) and in a great final of the then Cup (called the John Player Cup) against Rosslyn Park which they won 28-12. Derek was on the bench against Scotland at Twickenham and made the England tour to Australia in the summer of 1975. Eventually, he gained a sub's cap for the England game against Scotland at Murrayfield in 1976 and scored four tries for an England XV against America before being dropped for the Five Nations.

In 1978, Derek moved to the West Country and joined Bath where he had three seasons before going up to Oxford as an old man of 32 to do research. He was able to sneak a Blue in the centenary Varsity Match in the snow.

Somewhere in between all this, he played on two Barbarian tours to Wales at Easter and started his love affair with the Penguins, touring with them to Russia,

Argentina and Brazil. The Penguins is an invitation side founded by two stalwarts from Sidcup RFC, Tony Mason and Alan Wright. Their first overseas tour was to Sweden in the 1958/9 season where they picked up the name. Since then, they could almost certainly claim the accolade of being the most travelled sporting club in the world. They have toured Poland, the former Czechoslovakia, Romania, Hungary and China as well as several other emerging rugby nations.

While at Oxford, Derek began writing for *The Times* and the *Observer*, and chanced his arm at freelance journalism, leading to publishing and subsequently television. During this time, he was a selector to England Students, coached Richmond and wrote for *Rugby World* and occasionally for the broadsheets, and for two years covered rugby for the *Financial Times*.

Rugby has been in Derek's blood for 40 years. On becoming an MP in 1997, he set about reforming the All-Party Rugby Union Group, of which he is Chairman. Since 2001, he has also acted as an adviser to the Sports Minister on rugby and, in June 2003, the first rugby summit was held with executives from three of the four Home Unions and the Sports Ministers or their advisers. Issues such as immigration, visas, lottery distribution, honours, charitable status and tax were debated. In September 2003, before the teams fly out to Australia, the first All-Party Rugby Awards dinner will be held.

Derek is also the author of *100 Years of Ashford Rugby Club* (1986), *Wisecracks from the Movies* (1987), *International Rugby Alamanac 1994* (1993), *International*

Rugby Alamanac 1995 (1994), *Rugby DisUnion* (1995). He is a trustee of the Major Stanley's committee at Oxford University RUFC and remains on the executive committee of the Penguins International RFC.

INTRODUCTION

Most games that go open – soccer, golf, cricket, tennis, athletics and now rugby union – have a period that, in retrospect, no one is very proud of. It's that grubby period, that grey area, that shaming of shamateurism, that bit where players are paid in brown envelopes or under a table or behind a bar or in their boots. It's all a bit dirty but all sports go through it until they can resolve the transition from a truly amateur to a truly professional organisation.

There's no easy way and it takes time. The great players and entertainers of the late 1960s and early 1970s like Barry John, Mike Gibson, Gareth Edwards, David Duckham and Phil Bennett were calling for the game to make allowances or, in some cases, make *more* allowances, so that they could balance family life with work and rugby. It was not to be. Then, corporations like Adidas, Puma and Pony – some of whom had cut their teeth on other sports which had subsequently gone open – began to go beyond just providing free gear to wear, they began to pay for players to wear their kit, knowing it was illegal. They'd done it before; they knew both the ropes and the risks. Thus was born the Adidas boot controversy in 1982, which the English Rugby Football Union failed to tackle.

In the mid- to late-1980s, global sports television companies began to emerge. WHSmith, the high-street retailer, decided unwisely for its shareholders to invest heavily in Screensport. The European, largely French media players began to play with an idea called Eurosport. In 1988, Rupert Murdoch launched Sky TV with its Sky Sport, which was shortly followed by British Satellite Broadcasting's 'squarial' and another set of sports channels. The UK cable stations launched WireTV in 1994, which had started to develop into SportWire, a cable-only sports channel, by 1995. Elsewhere, America had ESPN and then ESPN 2, a classic sports channel and even a dedicated golf channel. Meanwhile, the Mexicans, South Africans and Italians had worked out that it is sometimes also helpful to own the stadiums themselves. Sport had become the preferred media for advertisers and sponsors looking for a global audience. Rugby was clearly ripe for the reaping.

It's not possible to move seamlessly from amateur to professional overnight. If the players are ready, the organisation that supports them is not. Interestingly, it has always been the player, the producer of the goods, who has caused sports to go open. Rugby union walked this tightrope between the players wanting to be paid and their Rugby Unions having their collective heads in the sand for much of the late 1980s and early 1990s. We have charted some of the main developments in this book.

And we use the words 'main developments' deliberately. We are acutely aware that everyone involved in rugby, at whatever level, has their own opinion and perspective on the events which shaped the professional game. We have endeavoured, as far as possible, to incorporate this range of opinion, and to identify the significant moments and decision-makers. To avoid *The Rugby Revolution* running to three volumes, we have focused deliberately on these key areas, canvassed opinion from authorities in the game and used the consensus view wherever necessary. Everyone's experience of the events surrounding the game's move from amateurism to professionalism will have been different, and we anticipate lively debate in clubs and bars wherever a love of rugby is to be found.

In essence, the two worlds of the players and the media owners collided and the game went open without any notice, any planning, any thought for the structure of the game in either the Southern or Northern hemispheres one fateful day in August 1995, barely a month after one of the greatest World Cups the rugby world had ever seen.

A rugby revolution?

A rugby revolution, indeed.

1

FOUR
MUSKETEERS

Four people changed the world of rugby union. A fifth, through an intermediary, tried to hijack it.

Amazingly, all their journeys to change the face of rugby began at the front end of 1995. Equally amazing was that they all shared the same hotel in Sandton, Johannesburg, during the Rugby World Cup in South Africa, where one party had announced its coup whilst the other was still desperately trying to shore theirs up.

The five people were Sam Chisholm, Michael Watt, Ian Frykberg, Jim Fitzmaurice and Ross Turnbull (acting for Kerry Packer). Sam and Michael are Kiwis by birth, with Watt becoming a naturalised Brit; Ian and Ross are Aussies. Sam had spent some time making his reputation in Australia, and Michael was an eclectic international businessman, firstly in the oil business where he made a heady start, and then in the world of sports management.

Watt is no doubt one of the most interesting characters in sports television. Before his move into the area of sports rights he was involved in personal client management, having a stable of clients which included Formula 1 drivers Alan Jones and Nigel Mansell, cricketer Imran Khan and jockey Lester Piggott. He moved on from there into the media side, representing rights to events such as the Winter Games in 1980. He makes no bones of the fact that he tried to emulate Mark McCormack's IMG, but, unlike McCormack, who became the world leader in golf and tennis, Watt went after cricket and rugby. It is not an exaggeration to say that he revolutionised the media rights opportunities in these two sports. Ironically, he started with rugby league, and along with McCormack he increased the value of broadcasting rights in a number of sports by many hundreds of percent. At one time, his company CSI Limited (Communications Services International), a predominantly media rights company, dealt with all the Five Nations rugby, and all the other major international Rugby Unions, Italian soccer, English cricket and indeed most cricket boards around the world. He made his money by giving guarantees up front and selling wisely to media companies abroad. His erstwhile rival at IMG/TWI, Mark McCormack, seemed ponderous and out of touch by comparison, and he wasn't as financially ambitious as the four

Adidas sisters who owned ISL in Lucerne, which ultimately went into receivership in 2001.

CSI was the global agent for the ARU for TV rights outside Australia from 1991 to 1994. This covered games played in Australia under the direct control of the ARU and televised in Australia by the Channel 10 network. Michael Watt subsequently built a close relationship with the QRU and was a main contributor of funds to enable the completion of a major stand development at the QRU ground, Ballymore in Brisbane, which opened during the International Series against Scotland in 1992.

A few years ago, CSI was sold to Interpublic, an American Advertising Agency, in a multi-million-pound deal. Watt stayed on as Chairman but not before he had dispensed of some of his largesse in various ways around the world. Helping Queensland rugby to fund a stand was one example of this, providing large donations to international environmental organisations and operating in quiet patronage of the Durham Miners' Gala in the North of England were others. Today he is a producer of Broadway and West End shows such as *We Will Rock You* and *Gypsy* on Broadway.

Frykberg had arrived from Australia to become Head of News at Sky TV in the early part of 1993. He lived in Knightsbridge and drank at one or two favourite pubs in Sloane Street, though he was based in Isleworth where Sky's HQ had been established in 1988.

Rupert Murdoch makes few mistakes and, when he does, he acknowledges them quickly. But he made one at Sky. He brought in a new and completely inexperienced Managing Director under Sam Chisholm in 1993.

Sam Chisholm is no more than 5ft 7in in his stockinged feet. A tough Kiwi who more than pulls his weight in any argument, he has piercing eyes and is not the sort of person to take on without accepting the likely outcome ... which is a metaphorical bloody nose. He is a very hard taskmaster who will not accept anything less than perfection. He is famed for his strong negotiating skills and has worked for both Murdoch and Packer. He negotiated the Sky deal with the RFU and has been involved in many of the major sporting TV deals around the world.

Chisholm had been responsible for bringing Frykberg, his colleague from Channel 9, to London to revamp the news shows, which were looking tired and staid even for Sky. Sam had saved Sky. His renegotiation of the Hollywood film deals when the company was all but broke saved Rupert's bacon. His skilful handling of the bidding to win soccer away from the BBC and ITV was masterly and helped create the atmosphere for Sky's successful flotation on the London Stock Exchange in 1994 and then climb quickly into the FTSE100.

Murdoch's companies work best when there is a judicious blend of Aussies and Kiwis (for their 'anything's possible' attitude), Americans (for their competitiveness) and Brits (for their creativeness). It is rare for there to be a Brit heading up any of his companies (though Tony Ball made a rare success of

BSkyB when he replaced Mark Booth in 1999). Looking around his UK empire, which included then the *Sun*, the *News of the World*, *The Times* and the *Sunday Times* (but not the *Daily Telegraph*, which he covets), he seemed happy with most of his Fleet Street editors ... except one. He was becoming restless with Kelvin Mackenzie, his editor at the *Sun*, and Mackenzie, in turn, was becoming restless with editing the tabloid red tops per se.

It's part of the successful chemistry of News Corp that the top boys and girls are moved at regular intervals either up, across or out. And so it came to pass that Mackenzie, with little or no experience of television and no understanding whatsoever of the fledgling satellite company in a car park at Isleworth, suddenly was made Managing Director there. Murdoch had taken a huge gamble ... and Chisholm had been left completely out of the picture.

Sam Chisholm must have been frying his brains when he heard that Mackenzie was en route to Sky. Here was a man who knew nothing about television. And if it was bad for Chisholm, it was worse for Frykberg. Frykberg, the consummate newsroom operator (television), thus came face to face with the consummate newsroom operator (tabloid) called Mackenzie. Mackenzie could ill afford to throw his weight around, as Frykberg had then a larger-than-life persona. Indeed, he was one of the few media giants who had stipulated in his contract that, wherever he went, he would have adjoining first-class seats.

Frykberg and Mackenzie fell out big time. Frykberg was Sam's man; at that time, Mackenzie was clearly Murdoch's. Sam had to look on from the wings as, sadly, Frikkers walked the plank.

Enter Michael Watt, who, if not exactly going through a mid-life crisis at the time, was feeling as though he needed a bit of a risk, just one more deal.

Frikkers and Wattie were not exactly made for one another. And it was some time before they edged towards an agreement that they should work together. First of all, Michael had to plan better how to react to what was coming. On the Murdoch front, it was becoming obvious to media watchers that he was building a 24/7 sports channel or channels that would need exclusive sports rights in each territory, as sport was the driver of ratings and, eventually, pay-for-view ratings.

In a lecture given by Derek Wyatt at the Edinburgh TV Festival in late August 1994, Derek said that it must be more than coincidence that Murdoch was building three distinct brands – Sky in Europe, Star in China and Fox in America – using two platforms, satellite for Sky and Star and cable for Fox. (He missed the connection in America, thinking cable was the only way to take on the might of ABC, CBS and NBC, but Fox has done brilliantly.)

'Moreover,' Wyatt went on, 'you will note that London is eight hours from Hong Kong and Hong Kong is eight hours from Los Angeles, which is eight hours from London ...' Murdoch, ever the visionary, was trying to reinvent the wheel but on a global, not a local basis. He was the only player in town with this foresight and drive, almost in spite of the costs, which very nearly bankrupted him a second time. The last time Murdoch came close to extinction was when a small bank somewhere in middle America threatened to pull rank on Wall Street for the sake of a couple of million dollars. It took a phone call from President Regan to the bank's president to save the whole Murdoch empire ... not a lot of people know that!

It was clear that Murdoch would need to move soccer in Europe to a 24/7/52 experience; that in the Far East, especially in the Australasian territories, rugby league would have to move to one calendar; that, therefore, the English game would have to leave its traditional winter/spring timetable; and that, in America, he would need to take on American Football and rebrand it. This would give rugby union a chance to go professional and then, at some stage, merge with rugby league (this prediction was way out) and cause cricket to become a secondary affair as it struggled for air time.

Michael Watt 'owned' soccer, rugby union and cricket. He always thought that rugby league would never prosper as a world game and that interest in Europe in American Football had peaked, even though Wembley had been a sell-out for the European Championships in 1993, a high proportion of tickets had been given away. The point was that rugby union was a sport in crisis. In our view, the executive committee of the International Rugby Football Board (the IRB) couldn't manage its way out of a paper bag.

The question posed after the World Cup in 1991 (held in the Northern hemisphere) was, if the Australian Rugby Union (ARU) had begun to create trust funds for its players, and top players like Brian Moore, Will Carling and Rob Andrew had begun to take on the RFU establishment in England, when would it go professional? This debate may seem to have resided only in the sports pages of our major newspapers throughout the IRB member countries, but a larger presence was coming to a similar conclusion.

In the end, it is usually serendipity that enables the last pieces of a jigsaw to be put in place. And so it proved. Kelvin Mackenzie did not last long at Sky. His management abilities were severely challenged and he fell out with Chisholm. Later, he bought into the cable station Derek Wyatt was running called Wire TV. Indeed, he paid £1 million just for the name and then astutely called it L!ve TV. It lost a fortune. Sam was back in total charge at Sky but Frykberg had flown the nest; soon he would be seduced to CSI as its new head honcho. The die was cast.

It is doubtful whether anyone involved in rugby in the Northern hemisphere – whether they were the Secretary of their Union, like Dudley Wood at the RFU or Keith Rowlands, the amiable Secretary of the IRB then based in Bristol – had a clue as to what was happening in the sport they were administering. How could they? They were dealing with a set of totally different scenarios. Wood was trying to fend off the likelihood of the game going professional, acting the King Canute figure, deeply worried that its very special ethos would be lost for ever. Rowlands was endeavouring to hold the fort and ensure that the next World Cup in South Africa hit all its budgets. In this, he had to deal with Louis Luyt, the combustible, red-raw Afrikaaner. Luyt was *de facto* the Chief Executive of South African rugby and the owner of Ellis Park, the main stadium in Johannesburg; neither task was straightforward.

Thus, the Anzacs hatched their plans to manoeuvre the game into becoming professional. The administrators (and the administrations they represented) of the three rugby-playing Southern hemisphere countries – New Zealand, Australia and South Africa – were sick and tired of the fact that they regularly whipped the Northern hemisphere countries at rugby when they toured, yet they had nothing in their cupboards as sexy as the Five Nations tournament. They were also surprised at how poor the 1991 Rugby World Cup had been in terms of the opening ceremony and of its impact worldwide. It had simply failed to make an impact. After the closing ceremony, the game just retreated back into its shell or, at least, it did in the North. In the South, something stirred.

Rugby Union in the Southern hemisphere is different. The game is centred on states or provinces. In Australia, given their extraordinary success, there are only three states that play union to a global standard – New South Wales, Queensland and, more recently, the Australian Capital Territory or ACT. In New Zealand, with a population of barely 3 million, the game has been cleverly structured using ten provinces in both the

North and South islands (Auckland, Wellington, Otago, North Harbour, Canterbury, Waikato, King Country, Southland, Counties and Taranaki), most of whom have whipped the Lions at one stage or other in their time.

And – surprise, surprise – South Africa has similarly focused its rugby on provincial teams, there being four senior sides (Western Province, Orange Free State, Natal and Northern Transvaal), and originally three secondary ones (Transvaal, Eastern Province and Griqualand West).

In the Northern hemisphere, only Ireland had a provincial set-up (which, wonderfully, given the sensitive political situation in Northern Ireland, has always included both the Ulster 'North' province and Munster, Leinster and Connaught, the three southern provinces, unlike its soccer counterpart).

In Scotland, former pupil or Old Boy XV club sides largely dominated the game. In Wales, the great sides of Cardiff, Llanelli and Swansea held court but there was also Neath, Bridgend, Newport or Pontypridd breathing down their necks.

In France, they had, like Wales, their litany of famous club sides like Narbonne, Beziers, Pau, Biarritz, Perpignan, Toulouse, Agen and the appropriately titled Stade Français, the only senior side in the whole of the north of France.

England was, to put it mildly, a bugger's muddle. There were a string of famous proud clubs – some doing well, some not – like Coventry (where they once paraded 13 internationals in the early 1970s), Leicester, Bedford (winner of rugby's version of the FA Cup in

1975), Gloucester, Northampton, Blackheath (the oldest club in the world), Bristol, Moseley (a once truly great club), London Welsh, Harlequins, Wasps and Richmond, and some upstarts like Bath, Gosforth, London Irish, Orrell, Sale and London Scottish.

The problem for these clubs was they had no power base inside the committee structure that bedeviled the English Rugby Union, known more prosaically as the RFU. Power was in the hands of the Shire counties – the likes of Yorkshire and Lancashire spring to mind – old historical counties but impotent when it came to rugby week in, week out. Until the power based was moved, English clubs and, therefore, England's success as a rugby-playing country were limited and limiting. England had the largest number of regular rugby players anywhere in the world, yet they had only won the Grand Slam twice, prior to the 1990s, since the Second World War – in 1957 and 1980.

There was one other element in the mix that marked a fundamental difference between the Northern and Southern hemisphere rugby-playing countries. In the north, Scotland with Murrayfield, England with Twickenham, Wales with the Arms Park and Ireland with Lansdowne Road owned their own grounds. But, neither the New Zealand, Australian (except Queensland) nor the South African rugby unions owned any real estate. Their provincial sides or a combination of public or private owners owned their grounds. Finally, after winning the World Cup in 1991, Australia (which had never hosted a Lions Tour of its own) was treated as an equal partner with its counterparts in New Zealand and South Africa

Bearing all this in mind, it comes as a small surprise that the Southern hemisphere rugby-playing countries waited so long to pull the plug. But, of course, the world was waiting for the pariah state, South Africa, to release Nelson Mandela from 28 years of incarceration. The apartheid-riddled country found itself cut off from trade and travel for most of the 1970s and 1980s as the international boycott on the country took hold. In rugby terms, this meant that South Africa could not travel to the 1987 or 1991 Rugby World Cups.

The 'Down Unders' made the move from amateur to professional gradually. In 1989, a competition was developed called Super 6. This included the actual provincial teams with two from Australia, three from New Zealand and one from the Pacific Islands. This was expanded in 1993 to include two South African, four New Zealand, two Australian and two from the Pacific Islands and became known as Super 10. This was run by a company which included the participating provinces and was managed by a New Zealand travel company. The teams were actual provincial teams, not composites. Super 12 was an extension of the concept – Super 10 did not become Super 12. This was the case put and lost in the Supreme Court of NSW by Optus Pay TV and the Seven Network in 1996 when they tried to put aside the agreement between SANZAR and Murdoch. Their argument was along the lines that they still held the rights (including global rights held by CSI) but in fact the competition and structure no longer existed.

The Super 10 was an unqualified success but manifestly expensive as sides had to fly to matches, overcome jet lag and play while seemingly holding down full-time jobs. It doesn't take rocket science to appreciate that something had to give. But, interestingly, none other than Michael Watt's CSI held the broadcast rights; moreover, the matches could only be seen on BSkyB back in the UK. Something else was becoming a major factor.

The 'something else' was not just the huffing and puffing of a gravy train or two. Ross Turnbull, the fifth musketeer, was trying to step on a few toes in Sydney, not that that was a totally new experience for him. He had played prop for the Wallabies back in 1968/9. Derek Wyatt first met him when he was on the England tour to Australia in 1975 and met him again the following year when he was the successful manager of the Aussie tour back in the UK, logging 18 wins out of 25 matches, with one international win against Ireland.

Derek caught up with him again in 1994 in Sydney, and then again in the Sandton Hilton in Johannesburg during the Rugby World Cup of 1995. In essence, Turnbull was playing catch up. The News Corp deal with the Rugby Unions of New Zealand, Australia and South Africa had been announced on 23 July 1995 at a press conference in Johannesburg. A few days later, the man who was dining out on double cream was none other than the *bête noir* of the day, the South African Louis Luyt.

You have to hand it to the News Corp team. a few weeks earlier, the whole world was in Cape Town waiting patiently for the opening of the third Rugby World Cup. It was going to be an absolute corker: South Africa against Australia, host versus Champions at Newlands in the shadow of the formidable Table Mountain. To cap it all, the great man, Nelson Mandela, would be there as rightful leader of his country. The pubs and hotels were buzzing. There were thousands of rugby visitors plastered in face paints proudly wearing replica team jerseys. Here at last, for the first time, was a World Cup in one country with no time differences and no currency or additional passport worries – a proper world championship.

Then came the earthquake from News Corp – a seven pointer at that. First up, the three Southern Rugby Unions had signed up to their version of the Triple Crown with back-to-back matches, home and away, for a tantalising sum of £370 million over ten years. This worked out as £6 million a match, a bargain. On top of which, News Corp had landed the Super 10 competition; it was easily the sport's steal of the decade and showed how little rugby administrators understood of the basic worth of their game. They would argue that they were the only game in town and that at £6 million a game, with a top-rated tournament to boot, they'd done a pretty 'bonzer' deal.

Nonetheless, the southerners had decided that, with this money, they could now assemble full-time squads and pay them properly. Of course, South Africa had been doing this for years, as John Robbie had explained personally to Derek Wyatt. Robbie was an Irish international who had toured South Africa with the British Lions in 1980 and liked the country so much that he stayed there. He has been there ever since making a very successful career for himself in the media, particularly with a morning chat show on prime-time South African radio. You have only to do the sums. The £370 million worked out as £12.33 million per country per annum. A premier squad of 30 at £60,000 a year with appearance money of £5,000 a game (say, six a year) would cost a southern union about £2.6 million per annum, so nearly £8 million for the three countries which, at £6 million a game, was peanuts.

If you were to take a different perspective, say, a salary cap solution at £8 million for the top 30 and appearance money determined per season, not per game at, say, £3 million for the whole squad, you'd be looking at £11 million per country or £33 million per annum, a closer call.

Even if these same administrators were looking across the decade and had drawn up their 'blue sky' list that included rugby centres of excellence or regional rugby institutes with second- and third-string squads and a full schools' programme, you would be stretched to spend the pocket money from News Corp. For on top of the broadcast rights fees, there would be a host of sponsorship and hospitality opportunities that should have doubled their incomes. No wonder they all signed.

During all of the negotiations, Michael Watt was

utilising his friendships and contacts around the world. It has been reported that Watt was in regular communication with the Australian forward John Eales. It is also known that he utilised his connections with New Zealand and South African players to gauge what was going on. WRC let it be known that they had a potential agreement with the American sports network ESPN. Watt contacted his great friend Steve Bornstein, the then President of ESPN, and reliable sources say that Bornstein actually asked Watt who was planting the stories that ESPN was on the point of signing an international rugby package.

Watt let this information be known to some of the players as there is no doubt that he (Watt) wanted the unions to retain complete control of the new professional operation and this was a loyalty based on the support and confidence entrusted to Watt and his company CSI during the preceding 15 years by all of the major Rugby Unions.

Whilst intense negotiations were going on at the Sandton Sun hotel in Johannesburg, Watt had another role to play out. Richie Guy, the then president of the NZRU, was being pressured by Jonah Lomu's management that if Lomu did not get a better financial deal he would be going to English rugby league. Frykberg told Watt that he thought the possibility of Lomu going to rugby league could jeopardise part or the whole of the SANZAR deal, or at least cause negotiating problems in the overall package. Some years earlier, a similar story was circulating about David Campese, and Watt helped his friend and the president of the ARU, Joe French, to find out the truth. In both instances, Watt used his connections and allies at the headquarters of the rugby league at Chapletown Road, Leeds, to find out whether or not there was any truth in the matter. Without divulging his sources he told Richie Guy to call Lomu's party's bluff, as there was absolutely no chance of Lomu getting a rugby league contract in England. Guy at first was reluctant to accept Watt's advice but as history now tells us, eventually it proved right and Lomu stayed where he was.

Murdoch's money had made it possible for the game to go professional. His team had done their sums, too, on the Northern hemisphere countries and they knew that France and England would need money, much more money, than their Celtic colleagues. And they were ready.

But before all that was the heady brew of the opening day of the 1995 Rugby World Cup when, aside from the spectacular opening ceremony and Mandela's appearance in a Springbok shirt, South Africa then beat the Aussies, Cape Town erupted and the ensuing party lasted all week. Few of us made it to bed that night.

When the News Corp deal was announced it seriously stiffed Murdoch's old adversary in Australia, Kerry Packer. There, Packer owned Channel 9; Murdoch owned Channel 7. Murdoch and Packer's fathers had been arch-rivals. Murdoch had done rather better than Packer moving to America, taking citizenship and building an edgy, multi-media empire. Packer remained in Australia but had uncanny nous with respect to the stock markets and when to move in and out. Packer has probably made more personal money than Murdoch, but the latter has had more global success.

Ross Turnbull, meanwhile, was bending Packer's ears, and probably the ears of some other investors as well, to do to rugby what Packer had done to cricket in 1978. Then, once again. it had been Aussie nerve taking on an Establishment in what came to be known as the Packer Affair.

Cricket, at the time, was experiencing similar issues – put simply, the players, though so-called professionals, were paid minimally for their success at international level.

Packer decided, with the support of some of the leading players of their day – like Ian Chappell and Tony Greig – to buy them up and play an alternative cricket world series. He could afford the former and he could show the cricket on his own channel ... but would the paying public turn up? In due course, he was banned from playing at the Test grounds so he simply built his own portable cricket wickets and had them helicoptered in. He was the first to introduce pyjama cricket and did what we now accept as normal – paid the players well, made the game more viewer-friendly and rattled the cages of the Establishment farts. We owe him a lot. Today, though, cricket may be in terminal decline as it tries to stop the onward march of 24/7 soccer.

Given that history and that quite fantastic success, it would not be unreasonable in your dotage to think you could do it again. The one real problem was that there simply wasn't the quality of stadia to host an alternative world series for rugby in 1995 if, as one had to assume, the rugby unions in the north and the provincial rugby unions in the south, stood firm. There were enough soccer stadia to hire in the Five Nation countries, but not in the Southern hemisphere. It could probably have worked in South Africa where there would have been support for a professional circus, but so what? It wasn't clear what the end game was, and Packer no longer had Murdoch's hold on the global media space.

When the story broke on 14 July 1995, midway through the Rugby World Cup, Turnbull claimed to have signed 500 leading worldwide players to an alternative championship to be handled by an entity called the World Rugby Corporation. We suspect that Turnbull had to announce something while the tournament was under way because Murdoch had stolen his headlines. But, at face value, 500 players seems just a touch difficult to believe. If the leading 60 players in each of the major playing countries – let's be generous and agree there were five countries – at best that's 300 players. However, in some of these countries there simply weren't 60 quality players to sign that were household names. Nonetheless, a large number of those players coming towards the end of their careers gave him their support.

Chris Rea, the former Scotland and British Lion, aptly summed it up in the London *Independent on Sunday* on 20 August 1995: 'It is hard to conceive of a more cock-eyed scheme than this one. It was a circus for clowns interested in only short-term gain and not the long-term good of the game ... Regrettably, a number of universally admired and respected players who should have known better chose to align themselves with this wretched venture more as a bargaining chip with their Unions than anything else.'

But the players at the time might look at these events differently. Brian Moore was like a lot of the senior players who felt they had been betrayed by the authorities. They had seen players being well rewarded in other countries and felt that, if nothing was going to change, then their only option was to sign for the WRC.

Whatever, the issue for most current players was quite simple – the game was becoming a major revenue-earner in terms of broadcast rights, in terms of sponsorship and in terms of paying customers through the gate. Most of this money went to the rugby unions; very little of it percolated through to the players. In short, the players would have joined almost anyone's army if there were a chance, however slim, of the game paying them something for their time and their effort.

For what it is worth, even if Ross Turnbull had pulled his scheme off, our instincts are that his major shareholder would have lost £15–20 million because he would not have had the support of the three Southern hemisphere countries who had signed for News Corp, and he would not have been able to recoup his money through broadcast or sponsorship rights. Turnbull created some wind but, ultimately, went out with a whimper.

And while all this off-the-field dealing was going on, the most successful Rugby World Cup so far was taking place. The opening game was the talk of the nation and there were other surprises, too, when Australia went out to England in the quarter-finals thanks to a last-minute drop goal by Rob Andrew. Then South Africa sneaked past France in the semis on a surface in Durban which would have been more suited to hosting a regatta, and in which France appeared to have scored an excellent try ... but it was disallowed.

If dreaming is allowed in sport then most of us would have hoped that the final in South Africa would have been against the hosts, South Africa, and the best team of the tournament, New Zealand. And so it proved. But, as so often happens, the best team of the tournament sometimes flatters to deceive when push comes to shove. Even allowing for the appalling sickness that some of the All Black players experienced during the game, particularly Jeff Wilson, on the day, South Africa just deserved their victory.

At the start of the game, Jumbo jets and air force planes flew over Ellis Park, probably below legal limits, but who cared? Nelson Mandela overdid it, too, but we cheered his Rainbow Nation even more; who else would have the audacity to appear again in a Springbok shirt? You couldn't help but love the man.

The game was about to change for ever.

2

LAYING DOWN
THE LAW

It doesn't exactly fly off the tongue but the world body that currently represents rugby union has been called the International Rugby Football Board (IRFB) for most of its 120 years. In the 1950s, it was known within the rugby hierarchy as just the IB; more recently, the IRFB has dropped the 'F' word and has become simply the IRB.

The International Rugby Football Board's origins were on the back of a dispute – surprise surprise – which surrounded a game played between England and Scotland. Scotland, unusually, disputed the award of a try to England from which England kicked a goal, which gave them victory. This was in 1884 and, because of the acrimony that this single game caused, England did not play Scotland the following year! No doubt, this gave a sporting credence to the 'auld enemy' legacy going back to Robert the Bruce.

A meeting was held in Manchester in 1886 without England being represented, and then another meeting in Liverpool in 1887, which confirmed the previous decisions that no international match with England could take place until the Rugby Football Union agreed to join the International Board. The first by-laws were adopted on 4 February 1888, but, as England declined all approaches to participate, they weren't of much immediate value! Eventually – a rather long eventually – England resumed international games in 1891.

In order to overcome almost three years of impasse, the dispute between England and the Celtic nations was submitted to arbitration. It looks to us as if England won the day, as the new IRB was to consist of 12 members with six from England and two each from the Celtic nations. The first meeting of the new Board on 5 November 1890 was held in Manchester, but there were no fireworks as all four Home Unions attended. The first honorary secretary was a Mr E A McAlister who remained as such until his death in 1897.

There was no alteration in representation on the Board until 1911. England then gave up two of its six seats and, thereafter, it continued with ten representatives until 1948, when England surrendered another two seats and allowed Australia, New Zealand and South Africa to become members with one seat each. The Southern hemisphere countries attained full status with two representatives each in 1958, giving 14 representatives (i.e. two representatives for each of the seven major nations).

The Home Unions had decided to abandon all fixtures with France in February 1931 over accusations of professionalism – *plus ça change* ... Eventually, France was reinstated in 1939 and international matches were played again with France by all Home Unions from 1947 onwards. France finally joined the IRB in 1978 when it was also given two seats on the Board. So the Board comprised eight countries with two votes each and these were known as the Foundation Member Unions.

The Board jogged along for the next 20 years resembling an exclusive white gentlemen's club with entry strictly forbidden to anyone other than the elite eight nations. Its objectives were very precise:

- Determine and safeguard the principles relating to amateurism in Rugby Football
- Frame and interpret the Laws of the game
- Settle all matters and disputes relating to or arising out of the playing of or the proposed playing of an International Match
- Control all matters relating to tours of national representative sides in which any Union is concerned
- Control all other matters of an international character affecting Rugby Football

A significant change occurred around 1986 when the Board decided to sponsor a Congress arranged to coincide with the Centenary Year. At the Congress, Associate Membership of the Board was established. It could not ignore that the game had developed and was being played in more than 50 countries. Moreover, the French had helped create an alternative to the IRB – namely, the Fédération de Rugby Internationale (FIRA) – and this beast began to make overtures to President Samaranch to become the officially recognised world body for rugby. Doing nothing was no longer an option.

With the 1987 Rugby World Cup on its radar, the IRB finally appointed Honorary Officers to conduct its day-to-day business. These officers comprised a Chairman and Vice-Chairman plus an Honorary Treasurer, in addition to the existing Honorary Secretary. Their new terms of reference hardly set the world alight. They were 'to deal with the day-to-day business of the Board and act in all matters of detail within the approved policies of the Board'.

Amazingly, there were no actual offices for the IRB Secretariat. It would meet annually on the evening of the Calcutta Cup. John Hart, a Scot, was its Secretary and his next-door neighbour took the minutes! At the time of the 1987 Rugby World Cup, the RFU offered the IRB accommodation in a couple of houses in Twickenham, which they owned. This coincided with the retirement of Bob Weighill from the Secretary's role at the RFU, so he took over as the IRB's Honorary Secretary. This appointment, though convenient, upset nearly everyone else on the Board. They feared a new permanent Secretariat would be too close to the RFU in every way; a move was on the cards.

Keith Rowlands, an ex-Welsh second row international

player, was appointed in 1988 as the first paid full-time Chief Executive or Managing Director of the IRB, although he was known quaintly as its Secretary. He lived in Wales and there was no way he was going to commute, so a small headquarters was found in Bristol, a sort of half-way house, for Keith and the Chairman, John Kendall-Carpenter, a headmaster, who lived just down the road at Wellington School in Somerset.

Kendall-Carpenter had played for Bath and England, winning 23 caps from 1949 to 1954. He was a member of the RFU Committee representing the Schools Union, becoming President in the 1980/81 season. He was elected to be one of the RFU's representatives on the IRB. Kendall-Carpenter was looked on as a bit of a maverick on the RFU Committee and, when the question of a World Cup was raised, he was certainly not against it in spite of strong opposition from many on the committee.

The Southern hemisphere, and in particular Australia, were very keen to see a World Cup and, although the other RFU rep (Albert Agar) voted against it, Kendall-Carpenter voted for it with the Southern hemisphere countries at an IRB meeting in 1985. Probably in return for his support, and to cock a snook at the Home Unions, the Southern hemisphere countries voted Kendall-Carpenter in as Chairman of the first World Cup, held in Australia in 1987.

After the Rugby World Cup in 1987, the IRB's ability to understand the beast it had created began to rear its ugly head for, although there was a small profit, it was in retrospect that they came to appreciate that World Cup profits could not be repatriated tax-free back to Blighty! By the time of the next World Cup in 1991, it was anticipated that, at various stages, the tournament would raise in excess of £30 million which would then be taxed at rates between 17.5 per cent and 40 per cent. Something had to be done.

The answer was the convoluted idea of making use of the tax-havens of the Isle of Man and Holland. For much of the period between 1988 and 1996, the IRB was out of its depth.

In 1995, a working party was set up under Eddie Tonks from New Zealand. The French pushed for a base in Switzerland or Monaco, but Ireland fitted the bill for most parties with very good tax-free concessions. The IRB now occupies very salubrious offices in Dublin. The peripheral offices were closed down with everything now being centred in Dublin and the IRB taking control of the World Cup and its revenue. At one stage, all commercial revenues went into the company in Holland and all income from the playing side into the company set up on the Isle of Man, but everything is now channelled through Dublin.

Change, even to the most conservative of bodies, had to happen as it looked increasingly to the players that they were more and more sidelined, and effectively irrelevant.

In 1990, a small earthquake occurred. The board agreed to a restructuring to allow associated Member Unions to become full members of the Board. But, as with the relationship between the Security Council and the General Assembly at the UN, in order to keep its exclusivity, the Board formed an Executive Council of 16, comprising the two representatives from each existing Member Union. However, it did invite at its 1991 AGM four other Unions –Argentina, Canada, Italy and Japan – to join the Executive Council, with one representative each.

It should also be noted that, despite the abhorrent system of apartheid then being perpetuated in South Africa, that nation was never asked to stand down from the IRB, as it had been by the International Olympic Committee, a further indication of the IRB's remoteness from the big picture.

The Board generally comprised elder statesman from the founding Unions who had served their stripes as officers of their respective Unions, and were then given the retirement job of IRB representation. The main activity of the Board was seen as inactivity, certainly by the players, who were getting more and more frustrated with the lack of progress in relaxing the Amateur Regulations. The Southern hemisphere was pushing harder than anyone for changes but the Home Unions, and particularly the Celtic nations, regularly vetoed any suggested amendments which might affect the status quo.

In fairness, there were changes made, but the process was more painful than extracting teeth. In 1989, another 'Congress of Unions' was held in November and, subsequently, a Five-Year Development Plan entitled 'A Plan for Change' was presented to the board. The Regulations relating to Amateurism were enshrined in stone and were difficult to alter under the current procedures: 'No alterations in the regulations shall be made except at the Annual Meeting or at the meeting specifically convened for that purpose and unless carried by a majority of at least three-fourths of the representatives present.'

One significant change, however, had been made to payment regulations 1987. The Board agreed to an alteration to the then Regulation 2.2, allowing for a Tour Allowance to be paid providing the individual's financial disadvantage was substantiated by a statutory declaration. The regulation was to be implemented or not at the discretion of each Union.

Regulations always applied to everyone and all Unions in their entirety. By offering Unions discretion, the board contravened its own by-laws, which required the regulations to be 'binding on all Unions'. Albert Agar, an ex-President of the RFU, and an IRB member, was incandescent: 'The decision to allow Unions discretion was no major mistake; it was a huge error of judgement which has seriously damaged the game. Discretion now appears to become the generally accepted means of reaching a settlement ...' and he went on to defend the RFU, saying, 'The RFU has been criticised, unfairly, for its opposition to reform, yet it took the lead in drafting the new Regulation 4, embracing a more liberal ethos. Unfortunately, the board went beyond the RFU's proposal in drafting regulation 4.3.2, which has been the subject of continued debate and therefore adverse publicity.'

The regulation actually allowed each Union to determine the extent to which it would adapt the regulation within its jurisdiction. It was the beginning of federalism. Agar felt that allowing the Unions discretion started a free-for-all with players from one Union looking over their shoulders to see what players from other Unions were doing. No surprises there then.

Agar went on to say that the RFU was disappointed and disenchanted with the Board's decision that Unions be allowed to permit players to receive payment for simply appearing at rugby functions. It had been suggested that some Unions might have been aware of the significance of what they were doing. Nothing could be further from the truth. The RFU representatives, in opposing 4.3.2, reminded the board that the RFU had put forward their proposals on the firm understanding that material reward to individuals would not come from the game. They called it a 'Charter for Cheats'.

Agar concludes, 'It now seems that some Unions have come to appreciate the full enormity of what has been done and wish to change their stance of 4.3.2. This is good news but their representatives had better have their shins well padded when the representatives from the Southern hemisphere arrive for the special meeting in March. Sadly, even if the RFU succeeds in its bid to rescind 4.3.2, it is likely that the Southern hemisphere countries will go their own way and the cry of "Foul" will be heard throughout the Northern hemisphere.'

It is interesting to read Agar's resigned frustration at what happened so quickly and, in his opinion, it took the game from that unique amateur sport that was strictly policed by the International Board to one that was sharply divided on its future and was no longer conducting business on a gentleman's agreement over a few gins and tonic.

Agar disparagingly stated, 'The Board was born in acrimony and, once again, relations between the member Unions are strained, on this occasion over amateurism. It seemed that everything was going so well following the decisions taken at the time of the Centenary Conference to meet the challenges set by the spread of the game throughout the world. At last, the Board was free to govern and was ready to act.

'It is not easy in retrospect to see how the present situation was allowed to develop. Perhaps in the fog of controversy mistakes are bound to happen. Is the lurch from the lethargy of the pre-1986 years to the crisis of 1991 due to woeful mismanagement? Arguably, the board today inspires trepidation even amongst its most faithful followers. Certainly, it must perform much better than it has done in recent years.

'There is no need to be entirely pessimistic. For instance, The System of Management and Control, which the board's Amateur Committee has prepared, is a step in the right direction. The hope is that, ultimately, in spite of recent setbacks, Unions will be able to work together to solve the problems over amateurism. The healing process must begin soon.'

Peter Brook became one of the RFU's IRB representatives in 1993 and grew as frustrated as Agar.

He wrote in an internal RFU memo: 'The world of rugby is close to anarchy. It is rudderless and powerless. The IRB wants the control of the Rugby World Cup. The Southern hemisphere want to rule the International Board.

'Money is the problem, because the players now demand it – not for playing, but for living and for work off the field ... and because of the enormous expense of running the preliminary rounds of the Rugby World Cup.

'Tax is also a problem because we want the headquarters of world rugby to be located in the UK. This is difficult to justify on the grounds other than historical – we have the highest tax rate.'

The RFU, in the form of Dudley Wood, the RFU's Secretary, who was considered one of the outstanding administrators in the amateur game, attempted to stem the tide. He wrote to Keith Rowlands, Secretary of the IRB, in late 1994 making the RFU's position abundantly clear on what he saw as the move towards professionalism which was now no longer creeping but had become an unstoppable avalanche.

He challenged the move by New Zealand and Australia to amend Regulation 7 on the admittance or read-mittance of former professional players. Under no circumstances, he said, could the RFU agree to a shorter qualifying period than three years. The difference in perspective, interpretation, culture and objectives were now so different between the two hemispheres that there was strong belief amongst certain high-ranking Home Union officials that future games between the Southern and Northern hemisphere countries could be put in doubt in future years.

At the Second General Meeting of the IRB held in Vancouver in 1994, 68 delegates from 45 countries were present with Vernon Pugh QC in the chair.

On the question of amateurism, universal approval was given to the Council to continue to fight for the principle that players not be paid to play. It was considered that the increasing indifference between internationals and club (especially grass-roots) players needed recognition, and also that money generated by the game be used primarily for infrastructure and improvement rather than as a reward to individuals.

Also at that meeting, mention was made of a 'Rugby Circus' coupled with the name of Jacques Fouroux, an ex-player and Coach of the French national side. The FFR confirmed that they were not party to any plans.

The Irish RFU had complained about the comments made by Louis Luyt, the President of the South African RFU, on amateurism. This started a flurry of correspondence between Luyt and the Chairman of the IRB, Vernon Pugh. Luyt made it clear that neither SARFU nor himself would be part of any professional circus and stated categorically that he was against paying players for playing the game, but felt other ways or means must be found to allow their players to play rugby union for ten months of the year and allow them to commercialise their names to make a living. 'I believe in the amateur game but I am not naïve enough to believe that the game is not threatened by commercialism.' This was rich coming from a country where major players were being paid, even in 1994.

A leader article appeared in *Rugby World* magazine in 1994 headed A CRISIS OF LEADERSHIP. It was written by the then President of the RFU, Ian Beer, condemning the board for their spineless attitude over the pursuit of those indulgent and grossly illegitimate payments to players. 'My overriding concern is the IRB's lack of backbone,' he wrote.

Beer had been with the England team in South Africa in 1994 and was invited to speak to an audience of distinguished ex-South African rugby players at a dinner before the first Test. He made a valiant attempt to defend the amateur principles and called on the administrators of the game to lock the stable door. The only problem was that the horse had already bolted in South Africa and, although he received polite applause, his audience knew he was asking them to defend something that had already been given its last rites.

In the same leader, there was also a comment on the weak handling by the board of the issue concerning former rugby league players wishing to play union once again. The article asserted, 'The laws are clear – no one can be readmitted once they have taken the professional shilling. Fine, except that rank abuse of the ruling is occurring and has occurred in certain countries for a considerable period of time. The IRB, preferring the approach of appeasement, did nothing. Now, of course, the genie is out of the bottle. The Australian Brett Papworth [a former League player] has completely flouted the laws of the game by forcing the Australian Rugby Union to allow him to play Union once again, under the threat of court action. Others are aware of the vacuum of leadership, which exists. The President of the International Olympic Committee, Juan Samaranch, recently promised that rugby union would be included in the 2000 Sydney Olympics. Samaranch added just one rider: he wanted to deal with FIRA, the European rugby organisation and not the IRB. 'The latter,' he said, 'was an organisation solely for British nations.'

'If a sport's so-called international governing body has ever received a bigger plate of custard pie full in its face, then we cannot recall it. The sadness is that the IRB deserves it.'

In January 1997, it was announced that Vernon Pugh QC of Wales had been elected Chairman of the IRB Council and Rob Fisher of New Zealand was to be the new Vice-Chairman. This was another departure from tradition as the Chairman had always taken the position by a rotation system. Keith Rowlands retired after eight years as Secretary in March 1996. Vernon Pugh became the IRB's first independent Chairman and then dominated the game for the period from 1996 until his death from cancer in April 2003.

Pugh was born on 5 July 1945 in Carmarthenshire. A coal miner's son, he went to the local grammar school, won a place at the University of Wales, Aberystwyth, and then went on to Downing, Cambridge, to read Law. He played as a centre for a number of sides including

Leicester, Pontypridd and Cardiff High School Old Boys and, on finishing playing, he took up coaching.

He was called to the Bar in Lincoln's Inn in 1969, and took silk in 1986, passing up an invitation to become a High Court Judge because of his interest in rugby. Pugh came into prominence in Welsh rugby in 1989 when the WRU ask him to write a report on Welsh players and committee members who joined an international squad celebrating the centenary of the Rugby Board of South Africa. Pugh issued his report and added an addendum criticising the WRU for not being up to running the game in the modern era.

Nothing happened until 1993 when the private addendum was leaked and all hell broke loose. There was a vote of 'no confidence' in the committee which led to a new committee being elected with a number of casualties from the old committee not being reinstated. Pugh stood for election and was then elected chairman, a position he held until 1997 by which time he had become the first elected Chairman of the IRB.

During his time as Chairman, he had severe differences of opinion with England and the Southern hemisphere countries on a number of issues, but no one ever disputed that he had a brilliant mind.

The IRB was receiving plenty of criticism, but in 1996 it had opened the door to the Dublin office in St Stephen's Green. At the same time, Tom Wacker was appointed as IRB's Secretary and CEO. Tom, American-born, was a senior investment banker and former player. For over 100 years, the governing body of rugby had been based in

England and now it had moved to Ireland with a multinational staff. The UK Government missed a trick in not keeping the IRB in London as it has subsequently done with the Commonwealth Games Federation.

Wacker came with high praise from Vernon Pugh. 'Mr Wacker combines a keen commercial mind with a great love for the game of Rugby Football. He is an exceptionally gifted manager and planner. I am certain that his appointment as the new IRB Chief Executive will prove a great success.'

For all the praise from Pugh, Wacker did not last long (only a year) giving way to Stephen Baines in July 1998.

Baines was born in the UK, had a Masters Degree in Recreation Administration from the University of Oregon, and worked in London and Australia before becoming Executive Director of the Canadian Rugby Union in 1975, a position he held for six years as the world's youngest professional rugby administrator at 28 years of age.

Baines had previously been the first Chief Executive of the English Hockey Association and he took up his position in Dublin in late July 1998. At the time, Pugh commented, 'The IRB is very pleased to have secured the service of an experienced and highly regarded sports administrator. The position represents wonderful opportunities together with some difficult challenges. In Stephen, we believe we have just the right person to head up the executive arm of the board.'

You can almost guess the rest. He didn't last long either. It goes with the job. It must be coincidental that two Chief

Executives, who came with glowing plaudits, fell out so quickly with Vernon Pugh. Of course, Pugh was always going to be the Chief Executive. The new CEO, to the astonishment of the UK media circus, is Mike Miller, previously Head of Sport at both the BBC and Channel 4. Perhaps it should be noted that it was alleged he had worked with Vernon Pugh before being appointed.

In April 1998, the IRB became involved with the problems and issues relating to the English First Division Clubs (EFDR). In a press release, the board commented, 'The International Rugby Board (IRB), the game's worldwide governing body, will mount the most vigorous opposition to a challenge by the member clubs from English First Division Rugby (EFDR) to its governance of the sport.

'The 12 English professional clubs in EFDR have prepared an Application to the European Commission in Brussels with respect to the board's by-laws and regulations on the release of players for international and senior representative duty and on cross-border competitions.' The clubs were challenging the authority of England's Rugby Football Union at the same time in Europe.

The IRB noted that it expected the RFU to adopt a precisely similar position in resisting the challenge to that Union's governance of the game within England. Vernon Pugh commented, 'If certain people are not prepared to abide by the rules acceptable to all the Unions in membership, or to try to affect desired changes other than through the democratic process within the

IRB and their own Union, then they have no place within the official structure and nor has any Union that accepts or accedes to such a challenge.' Decoded, this meant that the game of rugby was apparently above the law of the land ... which century was Vernon Pugh living in?

Meanwhile, Dick McGruther, a director of the Australian Rugby Union, stated, 'The rugby world outside England finds it difficult to comprehend why the problems caused by such a small group of individuals, whose declared intent is to destroy the existing governance of the game, has not been resolved.

'The IRB and its member Unions have been excessively patient in allowing the RFU sufficient time to achieve management of its internal affairs. It is also concerning to find the RFU in discussion with clubs whose declared aims are so clearly and unequivocally contrary to that of the Union's Constitution and the IRB's position. When your constituent members are taking action against you, it is time to govern.

'There is no room for fudging these issues or doing anything other than ensuring unequivocal compliance with the IRB's regulations – if there is a serious or continuing breach on the part of any Union in respect of the IRB regulation, then that Union puts at risk its membership of the IRB and all the privileges that are attached to it.'

The Executive Committee noted that the reports of the EFDR position indicated a full challenge to the authority of the IRB on some fundamental issues central to their government of the game, namely:

- Eligibility of players for national representative teams
- The primacy of player contract
- The rights and powers to regulate international and/or cross-Union competitions
- The control of broadcast rights fees

The RFU's lawyers had prepared a report for the RFU for internal consumption but somehow it was leaked to the IRB, and the RFU was summoned to Dublin to answer the charge of bringing the game into disrepute. They were questioned on a whole range of issues and were subsequently fined £40,000, with £40,000 suspended. In the end the clubs withdrew their application to the Commission when they received a number of concessions with regard to the European Cup. JP Lux of France replaced Tom Kiernan as chairman, the clubs were given one more place in the European Cup and an improved share of the money, based on the number of clubs and not on Union representation.

Touble had been brewing between the IRB and its French rival, FIRA, represented respectively by the board Chairman, Vernon Pugh, and the FIRA President, Albert Ferrasse. But on 5 November 1994, under the terms of an accord which was signed, FIRA withdrew their application for recognition by the International Olympic Committee (IOC) and indicated their support for the recognition of the IRB as the official international federation for rugby under the International Olympic Committee charter. The accord also acknowledged another very important step in the implementation of the IRB Strategic Plan for the future development of world rugby. FIRA was accepted into membership of the board as the first of its regional groupings.

As the IRB press statement declared: 'The accord represents an historic step for the IRB in its control and management of rugby worldwide and the end of any suggestion of FIRA being an alternative world organisation.'

At a ceremony in Cardiff in November 1995, the IRB was accepted as a provisional member of the IOC. Almost two years later, in September 1997, the IRB entered into full membership as the IOC federation representing rugby. We suspect that Vernon Pugh's head had been turned by the dream of rugby union being in the Olympic Games. When Jacques Rogge was anointed as President of the IOC in Moscow in 2001, Pugh was one of the few Brits to attend – and not one of the four UK Sports Ministers joined him.

The IRB just grows and grows. Already it has had to ask its two tenants, the Six Nations and the Rugby World Cup, to move out and to find premises across the square in St Stephen's, in Dublin. Ultimately, this means it is a black hole when it comes to funding. As a consequence, it will squeeze and squeeze the market dry because it is not accountable to anyone. More and more international organisations follow this path – the WTO, the World Bank, the IMF and the UNO spring to mind, notwithstanding the fiascos at FIFA and the IAAF over the years. Of course, some kind of accountability is built in, it always is, but none of these organisations is accountable to you and me ... ergo, the IRB.

Our wish is that the IRB should set new standards of accountability based on the notion that it is essentially a co-operative trust. As players and non-players, our subscriptions that we pay each year to our Unions should make us shareholders in this not-for-profit organisation and recipients therefore to its board minutes and decision-making process. The Internet enables this quite easily and with little additional expense.

As the IRB's location in Dublin brings it under the European Human Rights Act, it is to be hoped that, unless the IRB changes its role and becomes more transparent, players, their agents or trade unions and/or others will seek to bring such actions to make it accountable.

For the democrats amongst us, the idea that the IRB can continue to be dominated by the 'Auld' and the white Commonwealth countries by virtue of two votes at the executive level is nonsense. There is no real world government of sport – had UNESCO been established today, it would surely be UNESSCO, United Nations Education, Sport and Science Committee. Then at least the IRB could embarrass the IOC, the IAAF and FIFA, by virtue of the way it leads world opinion rather than follows it. One country, one vote is how the executive should be run with no vetoes, no glance to the historic past and a truly open body with all meetings live on the Internet.

Vernon Pugh died at a very early age of 57 years old. As Chairman of the IRB, he had his own unique style and vision for the development of rugby worldwide. The Chairman of the IRB has become a very important and influential role, not only in world rugby, but also in world sport. Rugby was officially welcomed into the Olympic movement in 2001 by the new Chairman, Jacques Rogge, and, as Rugby Sevens was played in the last Commonwealth Games in Manchester in 2002, there is no reason to say that rugby won't become an Olympic sport in the near future.

The IRB needs to elect a new chairman and this will prompt a very interesting set of political manoeuvrings. The Acting Chairman at the moment is Syd Millar from Ireland. Syd has been around for 50 years as a player, coach and administrator. He took on the role when Vernon Pugh died and the word on the street is that he finds the armchair quite comfortable and will continue for another year after the IRB board meeting in Australia in November 2003. That being the case there will be some very interesting political moves amongst the potential candidates.

John O'Neill, the CEO of the ARU, would be a good choice but under the constitution of the IRB, professionals cannot become Chairman of the Board, or even chairman of the various committees. However, O'Neill is campaigning to be the next Australian Ambassador to Ireland and if the Australian Union keep him on the Board in some way he could be a prime candidate.

The French Government would like to see FFR President Bernard Lapasset in the job, so he must be another strong favourite. Alan Hosie of Scotland is no longer on the IRB as he became President of the SRU in 2002. But he could come back as a candidate to stop O'Neil and Lapasset. It would seem that Bill Beaumont would not want the job, so any one of the present front-runners could come through, always assuming there will not be a dark horse coming along on the rails, as happened with both Brittle and Cattermole in their quest for the Chairman's job at the RFU. Watch out for the canvassing – the politics of rugby are alive and kicking.

3

LEVELLING THE PLAYING FIELD

Back in 1968, David Brooks, the manager of the British Lions, a side that was badly beaten in South Africa, voiced the view that, if the UK and Ireland were to compete with the Southern hemisphere, they had to have more competitive rugby on a regular basis. He was told on his return that what he had said was the equivalent to high treason. Yet, strangely, the four Home Unions delighted in selecting the Lions tours every four years or so and didn't seem to mind losing them time after time without realising why the home of rugby union couldn't match their former colonial cousins. Bizarre or what?

The problem for the bastions of amateurism was that a more competitive rugby environment would need sponsors, more commitment of time from players and a radical rethink of the committee structure. Ever the pragmatist, Brookie put his head below the parapet but, ultimately, let others wave the flag for change. Various attempts were made to propel the game towards more competition, but the amateur ethos was engrained in the officials and committees who ran the game. The telephone number of the RFU at Twickenham was ex-directory until 1986, the paid staff numbered less than the fingers on one hand and the Executive Committee had an almost Masonic feel about it. But it worked. Rugby was a leisure activity and, as the RFU had minimal costs, there was no pressure to do anything other than to ensure the accounts broke even every year. Internationals at Twickenham attracted full houses on most occasions and the game had that unique quaintness that the media found fascinating. If the engine ain't broke, why fix it? There were, though, occasional cries from the county 'shires' to have a fundamental look at the game and its structure.

For 22 years, from 1958 until Bill Beaumont's Grand Slam side of 1980, England only won a single Triple Crown (in 1960) and failed gloriously to take a Grand Slam. In the first 25 years after World War II, rugby union in England was largely a gentlemen's game, tightly controlled by the ruling authorities. Woe betide anyone who wanted to play rugby league. If you wrote a book and took the proceeds, you were automatically banned from being involved in the game.

Derek Wyatt, whilst a postgraduate student at Oxford in 1981–82, wrote rugby features and match reports for the

Times and the *Observer* for which he was paid, while still playing rugby. He was hauled before the RFU and threatened with the loss of his amateur status for taking money for writing about the game. Derek argued that, as he was a student, with no other income, his writing was his current means of employment. Bob Weighill, the RFU secretary, was flummoxed and suggested that Wyatt should join a trade union as though, somehow, this would ensure this was his only means of employment. He duly signed up for the National Union of Journalists!

However, from 1972 onwards, creeping 'shamateurism' began. It was much like a start-up company before it IPOed or floated. Maybe the watershed in the game was in 1973 when, in the last game of the tour, the All Blacks were taken apart by the Barbarians at the old Arms Park in Cardiff 23-11. It was, as the legendary Cliff Morgan was fond of saying, 'A fabulous match.' This game had come off the back of the first-ever successful Lions tour to New Zealand in 1971. The Baa Baas' game was live on BBC *Grandstand* and attracted an audience way beyond the rugby groupies set. Over 20 million claimed they had watched it at home, while another 250,000 people said they were there. It was simply the best.

The difference between 1971, when the British Lions beat New Zealand by two Tests to one with one drawn, and 1973 was simply television. The Lions tour was neither live on the BBC nor as-live, because of the time difference. BBC Sport showed edited highlights only on *Sportsnight* (on a Wednesday evening) or *Rugby Special* on a Sunday afternoon. Television was bringing the game to an audience who had never seen a live rugby game and, with this, came ever-increasing amounts of money into rugby's coffers.

There had been attempts to have a good look at the game and at the changes that should be considered. However, the Mallaby Report was rejected by the RFU Committee in 1973 and the Burgess Committee in 1981 fared little better when it produced its *Proposed New Playing Structure to Improve the Quantity of Play at Representative Level*.

Despite its rejection, the Burgess Committee's report was spot on, even if the RFU simply could not read the tea-leaves. Burgess recommended a 'club only' structure based on ten clubs in Premier Division 1, ten in Premier Division 2 and then national leagues below them, comprising ten major clubs and then divisional leagues, again of ten per region from the North, Midlands, London and the South and South-West. If the RFU had only listened then, the 1980s would not have been such wasted years in the international arena for the national side.

To get an impression of what life was like for some of the top international players, and the day-to-day stresses that had to be endured under amateurism, you need only look as far as Brian Moore, then the England hooker.

He came down to London from Nottingham at the end of the 1980s to play for Harlequins. Although a lawyer, he tried his hand at merchant banking and joined a company in the City of London. A typical day involved getting up at 6.00am, travelling into the City on the Tube from

Waterloo to Bank, arriving at the gym at 7.30am. A quick hour in the gym, then on to work. At lunchtime he was back in the gym and, when he came back to work, beads of sweat were pouring off him for the next hour.

Two nights a week, he would leave his office and travel to Harlequins' training sessions at Twickenham, getting home at around 10.00pm ready for bed. If there was an imminent England match, there would be extra training sessions. He was not exceptional, as this was going on all round the country, although Moore had the added problem of the London factor.

Wade Dooley was a policeman on the beat living in Blackpool. He played for an unfashionable club, Preston Grasshoppers, and was really the last of those players who came from a team well below the top dozen clubs to win international caps. His problem was that it cost him money every time he played for England, as he could not earn any overtime and he appealed to the RFU for financial help but it fell on deaf ears.

Mike Teague, the Iron Man of the side during the early 1990s, was a self-employed builder, and so also lost out financially off the field every time he played for England, along with others like Jason Leonard (a carpenter) and Mickey Skinner (an IT consultant to the Met Police). They were all proud to play for England, but the honour did not pay their mortgages or for clothes for the children. Those players who were lucky enough to be in good, well-paid jobs were literally subsidised by their employers for one reason or another, ranging from the kudos of having a current international in the firm to hoping that the investment would pay off in the longer term for the company.

Family life was also non-existent during the rugby season, when top players often had to play on the Saturday for their club and travel to Richmond on the Saturday night for England training at Twickenham on the Sunday morning, with those travelling back to the North arriving home late on Sunday afternoon, too tired to do anything other than sit in the armchair and fall asleep. If you were to add together the hours that many of them spent playing, training, travelling and getting involved in media work via newspapers and TV interviews, then this would add up to a week's work without even considering their proper day jobs.

In general, the authorities were unsympathetic. They had done it themselves in their playing days, so what was different? What was different was that, if you were invited to play an international in the 1960s and turned up on a Friday for a quick run-out session in the afternoon, it was, in a number of cases, to be introduced to other members of your team. And that was that until Saturday afternoon – no coaches, no physios, no manager. In fact, no one really took much interest except the Chairman of Selectors and his co-selectors. The President wished you well in the dressing room and out you went on the Saturday afternoon.

In the 1980s and, increasingly more so, in the first half of the 1990s, the demands increased with the appointment of a manager and a coach, plus other officials.

There were many straws in the wind that started

players feeling they were getting the raw end of a very bad deal, but more contact with other countries, especially those in the Southern hemisphere, convinced the players that they were being left behind. A trip to New Zealand showed Andy Dalton, the All Blacks captain, advertising tractors. A stop-over in South Africa proved that no one played for nothing in the Republic. It was all becoming surreal, but the Home Union Committees stood firm, repeating the broken-record announcement that the game was amateur and no player should receive any reward for playing.

This is what led affable characters like Dean Richards and Dewi Morris to become more disillusioned by the lack of understanding and why many of the players were willing to sign for the Turnbull WRC rebel circus in spite of their pride in playing for their country.

Given the severe demands on key players, and their growing awareness of what was going on in the Southern hemisphere, the Adidas 'boot scandal' during the presidency year of J V Smith in 1982 was perhaps inevitable, and had the RFU in convulsions.

The scandal came to light when David Norrie wrote an article in the *News of the World* in August 1982 exposing the fact that a number of players in all four Home Unions had received payment from Adidas for wearing their boots (£100–£200 for internationals). Adidas made a statement that the company had not made any payments to the players but their agents might have done so. Robin Money, an ex-Leicester player, who was an executive at Adidas, then explained that, since 1980, Adidas had been obtaining receipts from players in all sports in order to cover the legal position, and had warned them that they were due for tax on these gifts in kind and for cash.

The problem for England, in particular, was that it looked as though all or most of the squad were in receipt of payment in one form or another from Adidas or an agent. The players in the England team at that time included those who had been in the winning Grand Slam side in 1980, as well as others.

Adidas then changed their approach and announced that they had been obliged to hand over to the Inland Revenue the list of names of those players who had been paid money to wear their products. They admitted that the list contained English, Welsh and Scottish internationals but made it clear that there was no obligation for them to hand over the list to the governing bodies. They felt 'honour bound' to keep the names secret to help preserve the amateur status of the players. Adidas rationalised their decision by saying that, if they did not do it, other competitors in the kit manufacturer world would come on board and do it.

The Presidents and Secretaries of the four Home Unions met on 10 September and did what all good amateur committees always do – they agreed to meet again so that no decision had to be taken. In fact, the matter was not new, as Mike Burton, the England prop who is now a successful corporate hospitality agent, had admitted in his autobiography having received gifts and cash from Adidas, although he had denied this when the RFU questioned him years earlier. Burton was professionalised for his misdemeanours but, ironically, his book provided evidence that the boot money had been going on for some time.

England and Scotland ran into immediate problems, because of the imminent arrival of the Fijians. England decided that blacking out the manufacturer's markings on the boots would be the best course of action. Budge Rogers, then Chairman of the Selectors, was delegated to oversee this, but the good old committee system prevailed. Scotland were in delicate negotiations on a boot contract; Ireland did not think they had a problem; and Wales were not convinced that they could get the necessary support for the RFU's preferred action. So nothing was done, except to have more meetings.

A meeting was held with the Chairman of Adidas, Horst Dassler, in which he was questioned by RFU hierarcy and, as often happens in these types of witch-hunt, the accuser came out of it as the most honourable. He stated that he would rather lose such a contract and be out in the wilderness for ten years rather than break faith with the players who had been paid in the past by his company. Peter Yarranton, one of the RFU's officials at the meeting, told Dassler that his firm had created suspicion and mistrust throughout rugby and that, in their refusal to give names, they were putting their obligation to the players above their responsibility to sport generally, and rugby in particular.

Eventually, the furore died down. J V Smith, the RFU President at the time, said, 'It was rather like the Church authorities' attitude to the Seventh Commandment. You know that it goes on, but you are not keen to seek out the evidence and, when it is presented to you, action has to be taken. When asked for a comment, you say you wish it had never happened, and "Tut-tut" ...'

The overall irony was that Smith had discussed kit supply with two England players, Steve Smith and John Scott, a few months earlier and all agreed that it would be better for the Union to do a deal with one company and for the money to be put into a special fund with youth development being the favoured route. Whether the players were taking J V Smith for a ride is not known, but what is certain is that, even back in 1982, players were being remunerated, sometimes illegally, and the authorities did not have any idea how to handle it.

Sandy Sanders was an ex-international who played for England in the 1950s. He spent many years on the RFU Committee, was Chairman of Selectors and an outstanding Treasurer before becoming President in 1989/90. Sandy had always been one of the staunchest champions of the amateur ethos and hated what he considered the cheating that occurred to circumvent the Amateur Regulations. He is a very honest man and, although many of the players who knew him disagreed totally with his attitude, they had the utmost respect for the way he did not sit on the fence or court popularity.

When he finished his Presidency, he stayed on the Committee for one more year before returning to the far reaches of Suffolk (he could have stayed at least another four years) to offer enormous help to the local Ipswich YMCA Rugby Club which he is still doing today. In 1989,

Sandy was fighting for the game. In a letter to the RFU Committee, he wrote, 'I believe that the pressure coming on us from outside the game is beginning to have its impact upon the thinking of administrators in other Unions and we may see some proposals which will seriously differ from the present regulations. There is, inevitably, going to be a lot of debate within our committee and I am keen to ensure that the matter is given the attention it deserves.'

He enclosed an article written by Dudley Wood, the Secretary of the RFU at the time, entitled *The Last Bastion*, which was a bold attempt to defend the principle of amateurism. Wood and Sanders were like minds and saw the actions of the Southern hemisphere Unions (known as the 'Shu's' in unfriendlier circles in the north, or the 'Shu-ins') as threatening to destroy the culture and ethos of the game. It was a clever article, basically attacking the media for criticising those in the game who did not feel that they should worship at the altar of the pursuit of profit in sport. Wood wrote, 'The roots of amateurism in Rugby Union football go very deep indeed. It is fundamental. The defenders of amateurism are accused of being naïve, but they are not nearly so naïve as those who believe the game would continue as before if it had a raft of professional players to support. All of us involved in rugby football enjoy a wonderful inheritance and an enviable tradition built up over many years by dedicated amateur officials and players. We have a duty to preserve it.'

In 1989, the IRB published a paper on revisions they

were recommending in the Regulations Relating to Amateurism, asking the Member Unions for their comments. Dudley Wood was asked by the RFU Executive Committee to prepare an appraisal of the proposals arguing that the revisions were another erosion of a fundamental principle concerning the admissibility of rewards for playing rugby. 'If this principle is to be sacrificed,' he wrote, 'it can surely only be followed by the gradual progression to full professionalism against which there would no longer be, in logic, any defence.'

The IRB met in March 1990 and discussed the proposed revised Regulations. They had received replies from all eight Member Unions and two submissions from Associate Member Unions. Of the eight, five were firmly in support of the proposals, one was opposed to any change (England), and the other two were prepared to consider some changes. The revisions were approved but there was agreement that a new system of control should be prepared which would enable the revised Regulations to be interpreted and implemented in a consistent manner. England had set itself against the mood of change within world rugby.

John Mason, the highly respected *Daily Telegraph* Chief Rugby Correspondent for 18 years, saw the increasingly rapid drift towards professionalism which was given the impetus by the 1987 World Cup (although he accepts that there were signs well before then):

Little or nothing was done to prepare England for that irrevocable (and necessary) transfer to the paid game. To that extent, I believe Dudley Wood, plus influential members of the RFU, did not fully meet their responsibilities. But, of course, here, by and large, was the very group who wanted matters to remain as they were ... our great game, the last bastion of amateurism, etc. It was fondly hoped that if nothing was done, if convoluted regulations were passed attempting to safeguard the status quo, the threat would go away.

At the same time most, if not boasting, were then praising the increasing financial/marketing profile of rugby union, and England in particular, and making admiring noises about the length of the queue of would-be sponsors. In one memorable phrase, Dudley Wood said to those of us seeking an open fee-earning game, 'You can't get a little bit pregnant!'

No, indeed, you cannot. Unfortunately, he chose to overlook our desire for honesty, the end of hypocrisy, and an admission that the amateur regulations were being broken by all and sundry, the RFU included.

Mason felt that Dudley Wood should have been warning against the fact that you cannot shore up amateurism by selecting those parts of the financial package that don't appear to be in direct contradiction of the game's so-called ethos and ethics. In the latter part of the twentieth century, this was tortured thinking. It seemed acceptable for an employer to pay players while they were having time off for playing or training, and acceptable for across-the-board spurious touring allowances, kit and clothing, but it was not acceptable for the RFU to pay the players match or tour fees, or for clubs to pay or employ them.

As early as 1993, John Jeavons-Fellows attempted to drag the RFU into the modern era with a report called *The Administrative Structure for the 21st Century*. In it, he wrote, 'The challenge is to create a structure which can effectively administer the game in England, a game which has changed significantly in recent years. Whilst all around is dynamic, the committee and sub-committee organisation, and the way the game is represented on these committees, remains static. That cannot be allowed to continue.'

No doubt, Jeavons-Fellows's unpopularity in certain quarters can be traced back to this document which went down like a lead balloon. It was ironic that when the first club owner came on to the scene it was Sir John Hall, who took over Newcastle Falcons and became leader of the professional pack. Sir John would have agreed with a lot of what Jeavons-Fellows advocated, but he was not faced with Jeavons-Fellows but rather with Cliff Brittle, who became the Chairman of the Management Board in January 1996.

Sir John Hall came into rugby with a vision to make the North-East the Mecca for sport. He was the owner of Newcastle FC and brought it back into prominence when it was in danger of going the way of many clubs that were once great but are now languishing in the lower divisions without money and hope.

He owned the local ice hockey and basketball teams and saw the advent of professionalism in rugby union as an opportunity to give the public of Northumbria a side worthy of the area, where he believed there was a latent opportunity to bring crowds into Kingston Park, if not rivalling the soccer team, certainly at a level that had not been seen before in the UK.

He was a passionate, self-made multi-millionaire who did not suffer fools gladly and believed it's only the clubs – and it's the same in soccer – who will take the game forward into the twenty-first century. He got his cheque book out and recruited a number of top international players, including Rob Andrew from Wasps, who became not only a player but Director of Rugby. Andrew brought with him Wasps colleagues Steve Bates and Dean Ryan. He bought Va'aiga Tuigamala, the outstanding New Zealand player who had a spell in rugby league. Through Andrew, he persuaded a posse of Scottish Internationals to join and Newcastle were soon moving up the old Second Division to claim promotion to the First Division.

Hall had a vision for Newcastle, a vision for rugby and a vision for the growth of the professional game in England. What he did not have is patience, nor the understanding of the culture that rugby had developed over 130 years, and he was in no mood to wait for the old brigade to do it in their own time.

You could not have found a more opposite character to Cliff Brittle if you had tried. They clashed on their first meeting and every meeting after that. Brittle saw Hall as wanting to take over the whole game, including the international level. Hall saw Brittle as an obstructionist, a dinosaur in the brave new world and, in the end, both disappeared from the game: Hall to retreat to his Spanish holiday home and Brittle back to the Isle of Man to reflect on his 15 minutes of fame. Both, however, left a lasting impression on the game and, depending on your view, it was one of enlightenment or downright lunacy.

Hall could not understand the motives of the establishment. In an interview with the *Mail on Sunday* in 1996, he said, 'They are adept at holding on to power – who can blame them? The Civil Service has done it for years ... but now they have to change. It will take five years to make the transition. At the end of that time, I expect a Premier Division to be fully professional and the First Division, currently Division Two, to be part-time. I cannot see the game sustaining professionalism below that.

'The RFU has shown considerable strength of character by facing up to the need for change ... there will be a battle if they do not concede more power, but they cannot bring themselves to do it. They have an important role to play in administrating the game but the professional game must manage itself. They cannot keep all the power.'

This was seen as a challenge to the establishment by Brittle and his supporters and added more fuel to the fire that was already burning out of control. By 1998, Hall had had enough and sold out to a local rugby-playing businessman, David Thompson, but did not leave Newcastle in debt like Ashley Levett had at Richmond, and his legacy of making the North-East a vibrant area for professional rugby union lives on through Rob Andrew.

Keith Barwell, the owner of Northampton, summed up

many people's views of Sir John Hall: 'When the history books are written, the last five or six years will be seen merely as a blip, a difficult time certainly, but essentially just another chapter in a bigger story. What history will also show is that the man with the clearest vision of all was Sir John Hall of Newcastle. Hall had none of the sentimentality of those brought up on the game ... he saw it as a new professional sport, the biggest of the minority sports, but minority nonetheless, with a massive potential for expansion. We should have listened to him more carefully, but at least he woke us up to a few facts of business life.'

Hall's clear-sighted perspective of the game was that, 'Before 1969, there were no coaches, no coaching award, no mini rugby, a poor England team, no England A side, no England Under-21 side, no England Colts, no technical staff and no youth development officers.'

Brian Moore, the combative England hooker with five Tests for the British Lions and 63 England caps from 1987 to 1995 saw developments first-hand from the players' perspective. Moore, a successful solicitor, was able to articulate what he saw as the hypocrisy of the situation. 'Examples of endorsements, expenses payments, etc., were disavowed by the RFU as being non-existent, but it was clear that the Southern hemisphere were being given a freer reign to pursue commercial activities more than anyone else in the world. The "communication for reward" could have allowed a relaxation in the laws governing amateurism, but successive presidents ignored this. The English players realised that players in other countries were virtually doing what they liked with their Union's tacit or expressed approval, which seemed totally unfair as these players were able to train in normal working hours. There were always rumours in the 1980s that there were payments in Wales and France, but it became quite clear to me when we went to Australia in 1987 for the World Cup that something was not right.

'There were rumours in the early 1990s that there would be a relaxation and the players had meetings with the RFU officials at which Cliff Brittle said that he and several of his colleagues would resign if a relaxation of the regulations came in. This became ironic when he later became Chairman and put himself forward to lead the professional game in England. It was made clear to the players that the RFU, regardless of what other Unions might do, were going to construe the regulations in the tightest possible way. The players were quite militant and, after various meetings with the Willis brothers [*David and Bob Willis who ran their own promotions company*], a company called Player Vision was formed. The RFU proposed that they could look after the players but, by now, the players were so distrustful of the RFU that, at one meeting we attended, Jeff Probyn was wired up to tape the conversations!

'There were a few people in the RFU who tried to understand the players' views, notably Mike Pearey, a President of the RFU, but, in the end, the Willis brothers got fed up with the media and the politics as they were frustrated at every attempt to set up deals for the England side. At this stage, Parallel Media, a company involved in sports marketing, came on the scene and devised the "Run with the Ball" campaign. The players were absolutely up in arms at Dudley Wood's actions in trying to frustrate the campaign and criticising the company that devised it. The campaign did not make much money for the players, but it certainly promoted the game and the die was cast.

'Between 1991 and 1995, the move towards professionalism went forward at a pace in the Southern hemisphere and, when we went to South Africa for the World Cup in 1995, it was clear that many of our opponents were not in full-time employment. When we'd gone to South Africa the year before, the players there were professional but the RFU basically ignored it and still put forward the view that they were not interested in embracing professionalism.

'The Turnbull circus was outlined to me by others to be like the cricket circus. It became attractive to the players because of the intransigence of the RFU on any of the suggestions put by the players. I met Turnbull at the Ritz and he talked about three-year contracts; he said that the squads of the Southern hemisphere countries had already been signed, and that the co-ordination was being looked after by the captains in New Zealand and South Africa. I talked to the players in the other Northern hemisphere countries and certainly Scotland and Wales were very interested but the Irish were undecided. It was a very big move for many of the players and a number would not sign unless money was put into their bank account. It was a classic example of the chicken and egg and, in the end, the South African players got bought off by their Union and, without South Africa, it was a no-go operation. It came very close and James Packer came over to England to emphasise the backing of the Packer Organisation.'

The late Peter Brook, who became President of the RFU in 1996, was one of the RFU's IRB reps in 1993. He wrote a paper on RFU Policy in which he stated, 'If a vote was taken in the Executive Committee on Amateurism, I am sure all would vote in favour of it on principle as a bedrock foundation of our game. On the other hand, if you were to ask the same people if taking that line meant only playing Argentina, Canada and Japan, and that taking this line meant no rebuilding of the West Stand, I would hazard a guess that many would, in fact, support the Will Carling line – no pay to play, otherwise do as you like. What we have is mayhem. We need strong policy that we will stick to on amateurism, eligibility, movement of players and participation agreements. They are inextricably woven together.'

There is no doubt that the RFU culture was not ready for any major change and, when 'The Day That Shook the World' occurred, it was not a surprise that England was way behind the starting line.

4

AUGUST IN
PARIS

What happened in Paris on a very pleasant Saturday in August 1995 shocked not only rugby followers but most of the sporting world. Here was a game that had been in existence for over 130 years. It was played in over 100 countries, drew capacity crowds of over 70,000 to Test matches, attracted sponsorship that other sports would die for, had broadcasters fighting for its television rights and, in consequence, was considered to be a very lucrative sport – but it did not pay the players a penny. Or so it seemed to the average rugby follower.

Fans could not care less whether some player lived in a free flat, or had a sponsored car, or even if a star player was given generous expenses or payment for some extra-curricular activity. These players, and all others in the

UK, could not live on their hand-outs and had to hold down full-time jobs in order to survive.

The IRB had passed or 'relaxed' certain regulations which allowed various types of payments to be made to players and certain Unions, particularly in the Southern hemisphere, took advantage of this. The average rugby supporter, though, was much more interested in having a winning national side

However, money was continuing to come into the game at a faster and faster rate, and there were threats to the traditional game from all sides: the Packer/Turnbull-led circus, the signing of a television rights contract for the SANZAR countries with Sky for US$555m (£370m) over ten years, the threat to union players from the challenge of Super League in rugby league in Australia, as well as the growing realisation that the game's administrators were about to be faced with a possible almighty backlash from the players, if not a revolution. So the IRB met up in Paris for a board meeting which was to be the most historic in its history.

The meeting was held in the Salon Rabotin, Ambassador Hotel, Boulevard Housemann, from Thursday, 24 to Saturday, 26 August. The IRB Chairman was determined on a rotational basis in those days, and the reason the meeting was in France was because the Chairman was actually the FFR President, Bernard Lapasset.

The meeting included Council members from all 12 countries. The Chairman explained the manner in which he wished the meeting to be conducted and then, significantly, handed over the chair to Vernon Pugh QC.

Pugh took the chair and stated that the next three days would be the most important in the history of the game for at least 100 years and certainly since its separation from what became known as rugby league. The task ahead was a momentous one and the future of the game would have to be decided.

Most of the attendees did not come to the meeting oblivious to what might have to be decided. Certainly, John Jeavons-Fellows, one of the English representatives, had spoken at the final RFU Committee meeting of the 1994/95 season giving the Committee a resumé of what had been going on at the IRB. In fact, there had been a tremendous amount to report.

In October 1994, the IRB issued a paper to all Secretaries of Unions in membership explaining about the Working Party set up to investigate and report back on the question of the current Amateur Regulations. The Working Party was chaired by Vernon Pugh QC, with other members being Fred McLeod (Scotland), Bernard Lapasset (France) and Rob Fisher (New Zealand).

They flagged up the issue to be considered which was whether, in general, the current regulations should be 'confirmed', 'modified' or 'substantively revised and/or abandoned'.

They observed that, having already conducted significant investigations, the results suggested that at the highest levels in most (and possibly all) of the major Unions, the Regulations were not being observed. Individual Unions were either unable or unwilling to enforce the Regulations.

They concluded by saying that any set of Regulations put in place for the future should serve to reflect the nature of the game for the foreseeable future and, if the Regulations are restrictive, they should be capable of enforcement, and they should also be acceptable to players, clubs, administrators and Unions.

Then, in February 1995, the Amateurism Working Party submitted its report in which it said that the position under the current regulations was unsatisfactory.

The Working Party Report stated:

All members of the Working Party agreed that the position under the current regulations is unsatisfactory.

All agreed that it is not sensible to even further consider a return to the position prior to the last major revision of the amateur principle.

All recognised that the breaches of the current regulations are so wholesale and often representative of a considered assessment of that which is believed to be right for the game, that they are essentially incapable of consistent and effective disciplinary action.

All agreed that the pressures on and within the game were such that, like it or not, the game would invariably become fully professional if it were not better regulated.

All agreed that the present situation brought considerable and sometimes deserved criticism of our administrators of the game.

All agreed that the commercial pressures were now such that, important as indeed is the amateur principle, the major threat to the game is its potential take-over by those commercial interests. This makes it all the more important that we get right the solution to the amateur debate, which has very much the potential to be the catalyst for much else that might occur.

Members had different views as to how and in what respects there should be changes to the Regulations. In the event, the Report does not put forward any unanimous recommendation.

The Working Party, headed expertly by Vernon Pugh QC, produced a balanced report in which they concluded that '... We, the administrators, have brought about the present state of affairs ... in plain terms, we can only accommodate a game where the principal means of livelihood for the top players is outside the playing of rugby if we reduce the pressures on them.'

Another view, as they described it, was to reduce the playing period to seven months, limit the number of matches played by the top senior players, to impose a strict rule of 'no pay for play', but to allow the right to make money from outside the playing of the game, plus other regulations that would give the IRB a chance to keep the game amateur or, at least, not declared a professional game.

They obviously worked hard to give those doves in the rugby world something to hang on to, but it was as clear as it could be that the Amateurism Committee did not believe the game could be saved from the inevitable. The timing of all this, and whether the game would split again into diametrically opposed camps, were possibly the only outstanding issues.

Unions were asked for their views. In May 1995, the RFU, via the Secretary, Dudley Wood, sent a comprehensive reply from the RFU's Amateurism Committee, basically defending the amateur principle suggesting that 'It is not too late to keep control,' and if players wanted to get paid for playing they should join rugby league. It was a spirited response but really regurgitated everything that had been heard before in the defence of amateurism.

Other unions responded, including the Arabian Gulf, Argentina, New Zealand, Japan, Ireland, Australia, Western Samoa, Wales and Scotland. They all said, in effect, that the Amateur Regulations should be repealed and replaced with regulations which address the payment of material benefits, sponsorship and financial assistance, player contracts and player transfer.

Australia and New Zealand met together and sent recommendations at the end of July to Keith Rowlands, the secretary of the IRB, reiterating what New Zealand had said in its response back in May.

John Jeavons-Fellows, stuck in the eye of the storm, wrote to the RFU's Executive Committee in which he gave his opinion of what was happening in the Southern hemisphere and enclosed an article entitled PAY THE BUGGERS from the June 1995 issue of *South African Rugby* (the equivalent of the UK *Rugby World*), which was written, incidentally, before the Murdoch–SANZAR deal. The tone of the article was uncompromising:

Rugby Union is on to a very good thing. Just look at this World Cup, and then have a look at League's uninspiring equivalent. Look at Union with full stadia around the world, from the Five Nations, to the Bledisloe Cup, to the State of the Union clash in Australia, to a British Lions tour, to Japan playing South Korea in front of a full house, to the French Championship Final, a bone-jarring Currie Cup clash. The game ushers many, many more spectators through its turnstiles than League manages to do. Union is played in over 150 countries, 90 of which have formal competitions. League, on the other hand, has just three strongholds: Australia, the north of England, and Papua New Guinea.

There is no way that Union, with its greater variety and capacity to thrill, should allow the repetitive 13-man game to be a threat. But a threat it will be as long as you refuse to pay the top players. Union generates enough money to pay the top players very well. Payment already takes place, so let's bring it into the open and make the amounts much larger. That way, we can save the game, stop funny Antipodean circuses and roadshows, and prevent the formation of teams such as the Johannesburg Jaguars and the Cape Town Cougars. We can keep just about everything: the Five Nations and Test series and World Cups and Currie Cups. Sell all the rights you can, get all the sponsors you can, and market the game. Let the Lions still go on tour, but put the TV rights on the open market. Let Union actually go and buy League players. After all, they joined League only to earn more money, not because the game appeals to them or because the weather in Wigan makes it a great destination.

Jeavons-Fellows said that the article, in his opinion, sets out fairly the consensus currently held in that part of the world amongst players, administrators and the general public. Furthermore, he felt it probably represented the views of New Zealand and, to a large extent, Australia, although they were being somewhat circumspect in their utterances.

'Leo Williams (Chairman of the Australian RU) stated that some of the Murdoch proceeds (£12m of new money to each Union every year for ten years) would find its way to the players. He noted that it had been reported in the *Times* that New Zealand players were to be paid £80,000 per annum, with a lump sum of £60,000 when they reach the national squad; the Transvaal players were currently on strike for better pay; and the Welsh Senior Clubs had met to consider a break away from the WRU.

'I think,' Jeavons-Fellows concluded, 'before the August summit in Paris, the RFU faces a stark choice: (a) either create an organisation to enable our players at the top end to be paid (and risk junior clubs leaving the union); or (b) withdraw from the IRB, and initiate a new World Body, the membership to be controlled by invitation. This would most certainly exclude Australia, New Zealand and South Africa, and probably France and Wales ... It's decision time, and we have just six weeks. There can be no fudging, it's "a" or "b".'

Bob Rogers, Chairman of the RFU Amateurism Committee, made one last attempt to defend the amateur regulations by seeing if international squads could be separated from the rest of the game, otherwise: 'I fear that the IRB will decide that there is no alternative but to change the fundamental nature of the game for *the thousands* to satisfy *the few*.'

Bruce Hayman, the CEO of the ARU, sent on 21 August to the IRB the changes Australia and New Zealand wanted to the By-Laws and no one could interpret these as anything other than a proposal to repeal the existing laws. In four days' time, the show was going to begin.

The Agenda, which went out to the Council members, included the Report from the Amateurism Working Party Group with the Preface which read: 'The members of the Working Party are not in full agreement on the form of recommendations to be made to the Council. All of us share the view that changes are necessary to the Amateur Regulations. The differences simply reflect the extent to which we should move from the present position.

'We all agree that it would be unsatisfactory if no firm recommendation is made on this occasion. We had already detailed the options in our paper to the AGM in March 1995.'

So, 'not in full agreement', although 'changes are

necessary' and options already given in March. As they had said before, 'the one thing not on our side is time.'

The events between March and August over Super League and the Turnbull circus shocked the Board and it was agreed that, if the game had been lost, 'it would have been partly or perhaps largely our fault had that occurred'.

The Working Party Group put forward a very reasoned report covering the relevance of amateurism, the professional game, the choices, vision for the future and what should be done.

After Pugh's introduction, each nation in turn reported on developments in their respective countries. The batting order was New Zealand, South Africa, England, Australia, France, Ireland, Argentina, Japan, Italy, Canada, Scotland and, lastly, Wales. The late Peter Brook, who, with John Jeavons-Fellows, represented England at the meeting, made notes of each country's contribution.

New Zealand explained that the activities of the World Rugby Corporation (WRC) had caused a stand-off situation with their leading players. Twenty-three of their 26 World Cup squad had signed letters of intent and, in parallel, other senior players were considering offers from Japan. Indeed, the All Blacks captain had reported that the 'payment pecking order' was WRC, Super League, Japan and NZRFU in that order. After protracted negotiations, four grades of payments for provincial players and All Blacks had been agreed ranging from £26,000 to £100,000 per annum. Jonah Lomu had received special consideration beyond the maximum. It was emphasised that the contracts provided for payment for promotion of the game, but that there was general cynicism at the unrealism of this arrangement.

South Africa reported that the game was professional in their country. Twenty-eight of their players had signed for the WRC, including their captain who was the main recruiting agent. Most worrying was that many of their leading Under-21 players had also signed. SARFU had decided to match the WRC, which meant annual disbursements in five tiers of between £30,000 and £120,000 for their players. It derided the charade of 'payment for promotion'. Their President observed that it was difficult for players who could not speak English to promote anything in South Africa!

Australia confirmed that they had been at the forefront of the Packer/Turnbull attempt to disrupt the game, which, at times, looked like succeeding. They had spent much legal effort in persuading over 20 of their senior players to reject the WRC, and noted that their captain had also been a leading agent. In addition, they were under a serious attack from Super League. In the event, they had to concede to other players' demands, such as taking players as voting members on their National and Provincial Boards. Thirty-five players were now contracted, with packages of up to £150,000 for their leading players, ranging down to £30,000 for their provincial players. It was forecast that over 100 players would eventually be contracted.

England reviewed the current position, saying that they were in discussion with their players' representatives, and that the Committee had approved in principle a jersey sponsor which it was anticipated would provide around £1.5m per annum, 33 per cent of which would be placed in a players' fund, providing an average of some £20,000 per player. Contracts were being openly discussed, but it had been agreed that no firm agreements would be put in place until the outcome of the Paris meeting was known.

France observed that the WRC had concentrated their interest on the younger players, possibly because their top players were already well accommodated. Internationals received £6,000 per annum from the FFR, and up to a further £25,000 from their clubs, often as benefits in kind, such as jobs for wives and schooling for children. The World Cup squad also received £15,000 each for the World Cup. There was a firm view held that their players must be able to retain a job outside rugby, and new regulations were being enacted to prevent top players spending time overseas.

Ireland had been unaffected by the WRC, in that none of their players had signed on legal advice, and they reiterated their stance of 'no pay for play'. However, they accepted that there had been much movement away from this principle around the world and the reasons for it. They preferred the use of Trust Funds, and referred to their own fund which would provide up to £6,000 per annum. None of the provincial players was being paid.

Argentina were enjoying a stable amateur regime, with no money available for playing. They accepted that every country was different, and recognised the need to be flexible. They wished to keep control of the game in their country.

Japan had not been approached by the WRC and therefore the situation referred to by other countries had not arisen. They were surprised to hear from New Zealand of the salaries being offered (£120,000) to All Blacks to join some of their companies. Teams were being limited to two foreign players, and it was true that, whereas this regulation used to be taken up by first division teams only, the practice was now spreading to second division teams who were seeking promotion.

Italy confirmed that their World Cup squad had received £4,000 as a result of a contract with the FIR for promoting the game during the World Cup year. They were now controlling the import of foreign players, who it was accepted were paid by large companies for promotional activities – in effect, they were being paid for playing rugby.

Canada said they had little comment to make. There was no money in their Union and players were not paid in any form.

Scotland had set up their players' Trust in 1991 under regulations 4 and 5, but they had come to the view that this was now cosmetic. They accepted that that the game was now professional, and indeed remarked that they were indebted to the Southern hemisphere for bringing matters to a head and saving the game. They expressed a strong preference for player contracts, with actionable clauses in connection with off-the-field activities. They flagged a concern that money was not plentiful in Scotland and, consequently, that there could be an exodus of players. They would look to control this by contract.

Wales indicated that 45 (15 at Under-21 level) of their players had signed for the WRC, which the WRFU thought was never viable, but that the destabilisation of the game could well have been the real agenda. If so, it had achieved success. Several of their clubs were now fully professional with players receiving £70–£100 per week, and many being employed under the banner of Player Development Officer. Some Senior Clubs now had their own Trust Funds, and signing-on fees of £10,000–£15,000 were commonplace. Most clubs do not understand Trust funds, and have no perception as to why players cannot be paid. Clubs at all levels pay sometimes as little as £10 per match. Many pay only if the game is won. The WRU held the view that the IRB was now presiding over a fully professional game, however it may wish to camouflage the fact, and that, like it or not, market forces will prevail.

There was general agreement and honesty from Unions to the effect that the game was, in fact, no longer amateur in many of the Council Unions. It was agreed that Trust funds were generally a sham and that the payments were essentially for playing the game.

Unless the reality of the position was recognised, players would look elsewhere and for a game controlled and run by others where they would be rewarded. While most regretted the inability to enforce the Amateur Regulations, there was no prospect of successfully enforcing those regulations in many of those Unions.

The only honest, practical and consistent decision would be one recognising the game as being open where payment could be lawfully made to persons involved in the game.

It was agreed, amongst 19 points put forward, that:

- *in a majority of countries represented on the Council, the Game is no longer amateur*
- *the description of the Game as amateur is no longer appropriate*
- *payment should be made at any level of participation*
- *there should be no ceiling imposed on the level of financial reward*

Following discussion, it was proposed and, on a vote being taken, it was unanimously agreed by the Council that new By-Laws and Regulations recognising the principles set out above, be submitted for consideration and approval at the Special Meeting of the Council in Tokyo, Japan, in October 1995 and, following approval of such new By-Laws and Regulations, the existing By-Laws and Regulations relating to Amateurism then be repealed.

The only stumbling block was with the Irish who were not certain that they had the authority to vote one way or the other. It was said that nothing was being changed but repealing the current Regulations and the By-Laws, which was in the remit of the Council to apply new ones. There was a period of two months in which to put submissions or opposition at the next meeting in Tokyo.

Proceedings after the meeting took on a less serious note. On the Friday it was the seventieth birthday of one of the Welsh representatives, Ray Williams, and after dinner he was presented with a bottle of wine after which everyone went out into the night in their various groups for more drinks.

The vote was taken on the Saturday afternoon, with most of the delegates heading off for a few beers, and on the Saturday night, the French delegation took the group to dinner in the Bois de Boulogne and, after that, the drinking continued with a group of them visiting Harry's Bar and Kitty O'Shea's.

The press conference on the Sunday was conducted in an atmosphere of some relief and also some surprise at the IRB having been so positive, which was not an IRB trait. As Jeavons-Fellows said, 'It should not have come as a surprise because there were enough warnings before, but no one believed it would happen. This was in spite of a report of the Amateurism Committee in February and a meeting of the Council which was held in March to discuss the report. Within the report was a clear message of what was going to happen. New Zealand and Australia urged that the hypocrisy had to stop.'

At the press conference, Vernon Pugh stated, 'We are entering a very different world. The game will change for all concerned, including players and administrators alike. The challenge is to retain the special character which has helped make rugby so popular. The decision of the Council is an extremely positive and bold one.'

There is no doubt that the events surrounding Murdoch and Turnbull had had a profound effect on the thinking, resulting in much less chance of a fudge. The Murdoch deal gave the money while the Turnbull activities frightened the SANZAR Unions to such an extent that it forced them to allocate their money to combat the Turnbull offers, which otherwise they might not have done. It allowed them, and particularly South Africa, to match the Turnbull offer, and the other two to make offers that saved their game, with Australia guaranteeing their players 90 per cent of the equivalent Murdoch offer.

The French remained inscrutable – which didn't surprise anyone.

The news broke in full on the Sunday morning. Colin Herridge heard the details on the radio as he drove to the Oval to watch the England v West Indies cricket Test match. While at the Oval, he received a call from Sky Sports asking for a reaction. At the time, Colin was in charge of media liaison for the England rugby side, and had been since the 1991 World Cup. He explained he was at the Oval but Sky insisted on sending a reporter to the ground to get a reaction to the news. Colin, like everyone else associated with the national side, had realised since 1991 that the players could not continue under the present regulations, but also, as an RFU Committee Member, he had seen first-hand the resolve of a number of the Committee, led by the secretary, Dudley Wood, who were adamant that the game would stay amateur. He was therefore surprised that a unanimous decision had been made by the IRB without any reference back to their respective Unions. His surprise was shared by so many of those close to the game, let alone the rugby man in the street.

The reaction was one of genuine surprise at what had happened in Paris. Dennis Easby, the former President of the RFU and an ex-IRB representative, felt the Home Unions would never go along with professionalism, whilst France remained firmly on the fence, asserting that if a player was earning no more than £25,000 per annum, then he was deemed an amateur.

Easby is an ex-referee who represented Berkshire on the RFU. He was a popular president of the Union who will be remembered as the person who sacked Will Carling as the England captain after Carling's remarks about the RFU Committee being '57 old farts'. He was besieged at his home by the media and was fortunate to find a way out of his dilemma when Gary Newbon, a sports broadcaster, brokered a deal on air between Easby and Jon Holmes, Carling's agent at the time. A pipe of peace meeting was arranged between Carling and Easby, the outcome being that Carling had his captaincy reinstated in time for the 1995 World Cup.

Easby commented, 'I was very surprised that the game went professional when it did. I thought it would last another ten years as an amateur game. The RFU was very much of a mind that we did not want the game to go professional. At the same time, people were being persuaded to extend the Amateur Regulations so that the players could get as much as they could out of the current regulations.

'I definitely saw an increasing groundswell for the relaxing of regulations. The game had virtually breached the whole of the Amateur Regulations by the time it went professional. In my last year on the IRB in 1994, I suggested we should all come with a clean sheet of paper, open up our hearts and try and work from that.'

Bill Bishop was the incumbent President in 1995. If Bishop ever collected travel miles during his period at the RFU, he could probably have gone round the world free a dozen times with his wife. Bill came on to the RFU Committee representing Cornwall in 1976. He became President in 1995 and, in those 20 years, he travelled tens of thousands of miles backwards and forwards from the extremes of Cornwall to London and every other part of the UK, as well as many overseas trips on RFU business.

He played in the front row for Cornwall, is Cornish to his fingertips and chaired several very important committees which had a profound effect on English rugby. He headed up the committee that recommended and implemented leagues in the second half of the 1980s. The Bishop Commission became the foundation for the change of the RFU Committee in the 1990s.

Bill was a strong supporter of county rugby as befits any Cornishman, but he was realistic enough to know that the game had to move forward and competitive rugby at club level was needed to upgrade the standards of the game.

When he became President just after the 1995 World Cup, taking over from Dennis Easby, he was able to distance himself from the hot water that Easby got into for sacking Carling over his 'old farts' comment. However, he was to become the first of three Presidents who, by their own admission, endured the unhappiest period of their rugby careers when they crossed swords with Cliff Brittle.

Bishop was an honest, no-frills, what-you-see-is-what-you-get, old-style rugby traditionalist who could have handled the day-to-day President's role in the amateur era with his eyes shut. He was well liked, knew his way round the rugby world and, with Peter Bromage the elected first Chairman of the Management Board due to take on the more cerebal tasks of running the Union, Bishop was looking forward to his year in the limelight. The fact that it turned into a year of hell is almost an understatement. The death of Bromage, the announcement in Paris, the threatened expulsion of England from the Five Nations, the election of Cliff Brittle to the Chairman's role in January and particularly Bishop's battles with him contrived to turn the amiable, outgoing, jovial storyteller into a frustrated and disillusioned individual who could not wait for his year of office to come to an end.

However, for Bishop the decision in Paris came as a bombshell. 'The Secretary and the President were presented with a *fait accompli* and had to think on their feet which is never a good way to act.'

Brian Baister, who was to succeed Brittle as Chairman of the Management Board in 1998, observed that a number of the Council members did not want change. They were members of an exclusive club, and had their little committees to run.

Nigel Wray, the owner of Saracens, observed that rugby had an entrenched amateur ethos since the game split over 100 years earlier. As far as he was concerned, it had always wanted to remain amateur and always saw something special about being amateur. There was an upsurge of anger that the game must be preserved. It was a big change and change was not welcomed. There were a lot of people with a vested interest and power in the amateur game so they would feel resentment about what had happened. It was inevitable that there would be a long struggle.

Bob Rogers was Chairman of the RFU Amateur Sub-Committee, and was not impressed in any way by what happened in Paris. He felt 'the cheats had won' and did not feel that the IRB had given guidance and leadership on control of commercialism, player movement, restrictions on player demands, and protection of Unions' and clubs' financial interests.

However, in fairness, he urged the RFU to be positive and proactive. 'We must move forward, not back, and we should make the best of what is happening. The challenge is to be grasped ... Whilst we have spent the last ten years defending amateurism we must not spend the next few years regretting its passing.'

Mike James, an ex-player who became a successful businessman, was, at the time, the Chairman of Swansea. 'We, at Swansea, were not ready for what happened in 1995 and it came as a massive surprise, particularly as the Chairman of the IRB was a Welshman. He certainly did not have a brief from the clubs and it was a bombshell. In fact, the clubs had a small committee which drew up a blueprint for Vernon Pugh, and it was suggested we follow the model of the Southern hemisphere, particularly Australia, where the principal players were contracted by the Union and the clubs became part of the Union in the proper business sense.

'Vernon did nothing with this report because it probably affected the grand plan that he had, but which we knew nothing about. We were not ready for it. We had a turnover at Swansea for the season of 1994/5 of £400,000 and we opened the doors to the season 1995/6 with a committed wage bill of £600,000. We had been told that the WRU would be shoulder to shoulder with the clubs in the brave new world. The WRU had no preparation and it seemed that even Pugh had no preparation for the Union. It was certainly not in the best interests of the WRU and not for anyone in the Northern hemisphere. Clubs were left high and dry with the blind leading the blind. There was no considered business plan for Welsh rugby.'

Charles Jillings, one of the owners of Harlequins, stated, 'The professional game got off on the wrong foot. Nobody had a view on how the game should be taken forward – no framework, no structure. Some thought the professional game would fail. A big divergence in opinions. No leadership taken, no template. Everything based on emotion.'

Roger Godfrey, who was the RFU Administrative Secretary from 1987 to 1999, saw the reactions from a good vantage point. 'When professionalism came, the RFU was unprepared because one of the great administrators, Dudley Wood, had never wanted to accept professionalism and had made no contingency plans before he handed over to Hallett. A lot of the Committee was against professionalism in spite of it being inevitable. The Southern hemisphere did not have the "dyed in the wool" type of person as in the Northern hemisphere.'

Budge Rogers, who held the record for winning the most England caps for many years, and who became President of the RFU in 2000, was surprised when they made the announcement about the game going professional. 'However, I even saw in my last year as Chairman of Selectors in 1984, and before the Adidas scandal, we were beginning to see the players demanding more and more, but I was still surprised at such a big step.'

Brian Moore was elated by the news but not optimistic about England's chances of handling the change-over. 'Most of the players saw the decision in August 1995 as giving them a level playing field with the Southern hemisphere players, where some of them had been fully professional for four years. I was not surprised that we were so unprepared in England – it was as if it was "a plague on all your houses" attitude and the Luddites would not be seen to be endorsing any step towards professionalism. I rather likened it to the board of a PLC who saw change coming but were against it. However, if they left the shareholders and the employees without any plan to exist in a changed market, all that board would be sacked immediately.

'The players in the middle of their career had to weigh up what they should do with their careers but the inability of the RFU to put in any substantial framework did not help the situation. The standards have got better but the game has ironically lost a sort of quaintness where players of very different backgrounds came together and brought their own experiences of life giving a very interesting mix. Professionalism is a separate entity from the rest of the sport and this must be realised with a split between the running of the game but making sure that the amateur side is properly funded.

'What the rugby public cannot understand is the bitterness and the bad feeling that there was from the players towards the Committee and Dudley Wood in particular, for what they thought was spiteful and vindictive as well as hypocritical and dishonest. It is obvious now, but it could have been done much better. More than probably £80m has been wasted over the last six years by the owners who have been invariably criticised, but who was it who put their money where their mouth was? Think where we would be if that money had been spent wisely and properly harnessed in a co-ordinated way with realistic salary caps and projections.'

As far as the Southern hemisphere was concerned, many people said that the move towards professionalism was just accepting the status quo, whereas in the Northern hemisphere it sparked a virtual revolution

The situation was neatly summed up by Mark Evans, the shrewd CEO of Harlequins, who, in 1995, was the Coach of Saracens: 'Amateurism went out of the window that day before the Final of the World Cup in 1995.'

The scene was set for the most unedifying scrap that the game had ever witnessed.

THE STATE OF
THE UNION

In soccer, in cricket and in rugby union, neither the United Kingdom nor Great Britain fields a team, largely because most team games were 'invented' in England during the late eighteenth and early to mid-nineteenth centuries. Quite naturally, England then fielded teams against its three Celtic neighbours (Ireland being one country until 1922) before the diaspora of the Empire took the games further afield to Australia, New Zealand (the Scots), Argentina (the Welsh) and South Africa.

In truth, the main missionaries of these games were not the bible bashers or the explorers but our own armed services that have a proud place in the histories of these particular sports. It would be pretty cheap to suggest that it therefore follows that, because of all this, England is the country everyone wants to beat. We suspect that deep in the history of these countries, long before sport entered the scene, is both an abiding respect for the English but also an ingrained dislike – hatred is too strong a word – of its underlying arrogance.

This sentiment was summed up with some force and not a little insight by a French barrister who was giving a lecture on the importance of the EU, not knowing that an Englishman, let's call him Derek Wyatt, was sitting in the audience in Brussels. 'It was much easier when there were just six countries in the EU, because we French could go around telling everyone we were the most intelligent race in the world. And the English? Since the English joined the EU, they don't go around telling everyone they are the most intelligent race in the world, they just assume they are.'

If it wasn't bad enough being humbled on the field, it was pretty unpleasant watching the tortuous journey that England made of it on the road to professional rugby. In retrospect, it seemed that, following the announcement in Paris on 27 August 1995, England was playing a different game.

During its 133 years, the RFU, as the oldest Union, has variously been seen as founding father, leader of the game, dodo, do-gooder, patroniser of the Celts and/or just generally squandering its substantial resources on the playing field. As the undisputed founder, it has never thought to change its title to the English Rugby Union as a gesture of equality with the other nations, nor for the more practical advantages of marketing and communications – it has always been difficult to shout 'Come on RFU' at Twickenham!

Before the start of RWC95, the RFU had had five outstanding years. On the field, under the shrewd leadership of Geoff Cooke and the bright captaincy of Will Carling, England won three Grand Slams and earlier had reached the final of the 1991 Rugby World Cup.

Off the field, under the stewardship of the then Secretary, Dudley Wood, the Twickenham ground was being transformed. Much of this was down to Tony Hallett, soon to be his successor at the RFU.

Lieutenant Commander AP Hallett RN was a career services man who was elected to the RFU Committee in 1979. At 34 years of age, he was its youngest member and was still playing in the second or back row at Richmond while holding down a desk job in the Ministry of Defence in Whitehall.

He was at the forefront of helping to finance and develop Twickenham, chairing the Redevelopment Committee. He was appointed to replace Dudley Wood on his retirement as Secretary in 1995. Hallett was in South Africa for the Rugby World Cup as Secretary-Designate of the RFU and found out that 'something is occurring in Ellis Park tomorrow and you should be there'.

He witnessed the three Presidents of the Southern hemisphere countries make the announcement to a predominantly British press corps. Most of the journalists had focused their thoughts and energies on the strange case of possible food poisoning and had little anticipation of what they were about to be told – that the three nations had signed a massive TV deal with News Corp for the next ten years.

Hallett, as only the Secretary-Designate, had no official status there, so he headed for the door. But the British media saw him and a bizarre scene developed, with the journalists milling around Hallett asking for a reaction, while the architects of the biggest deal ever to occur in rugby had to talk amongst themselves.

Hallett stole the spotlight, particularly as he ventured the view that the News Corp deal could 'drive a coach and horses through the IRB's Amateur Regulations', and his comments quickly reverberated across the world. Little did Hallett think at the time that he would be one of those who had to live with the consequences of the TV deal as it killed off any hope that the game could remain amateur. His destiny was sealed only a month later with the announcement in Paris, and his generalship of an amateur sport was ended.

Hallett's team had completed the redevelopment of Twickenham with the most advanced interactive Museum and Research facility in world rugby. NatWest and Flemings had ensured the finance for the development of the stadium, and the sale of the third tranche of the 'Best Seat in the House' Debenture Scheme funded the remaining costs. Twickenham presented magnificence with a public and corporate hospitality cash-earning machine to go with it. The place was filled with shops, bars, boxes by the hundred, dining and conference facilities and an increased capacity of 75,000, all seated. The Committee's eyes boggled with a cocktail of pride, pleasure and myopia.

In setting the scene at HQ, before the up-coming 'Dogs of War' interlude, it is important to recognise the singular part that Peter Bromage, Senior Partner of solicitors Eversheds, played in putting the administration and finance in place. He was exhausting company, burned the candle at both ends on behalf of his company and the RFU Treasury, which he led with style and financial prudence. He was almost too good to be true; he advised on everything, he foresaw problems ahead, he was on most ad hoc sub-committees – the important ones, anyway – was in charge of forward planning and played a fair game of golf and a powerful hand of bridge. More importantly, he did not want the President's job, which in his view would take him away from the centre of business – he wanted and won the newly introduced appointment of Chairman of the Management Board.

Bromage became the Chairman by being voted in by a big majority of the RFU Committee following the recommendation of the Bishop Committee to have a Chairman who would take over a large number of the duties of the President. For what it's worth, he was also Hallett's strongest supporter for the job of Secretary and Chief Executive of the RFU in succession to Dudley Wood.

Bromage was a member of Warwickshire County Cricket Club Committee and Chairman of the MCC's Disciplinary Committee. He understood professional sport and was a firm but fair debater and negotiator, who was viewed by the senior clubs as someone with whom they could work, as he had already been in discussions with them on the distribution of television money.

The Rugby Football Union Committee (now renamed the 'Council', a rather down-market name but essential, nonetheless, to purge the memory of Carling's remark about the 'old farts') now could look forward to a successful period of playing dominance and sustained growth – improved earnings per annum amounted to £1.5m; despite depreciation of £5m and interest of £3m, it left a warm glow. This was July 1995, a month after the 1995 Rugby World Cup had finished, and the RFU's AGM had been completed in 48 minutes, a record. Everything in the garden (or cabbage patch) seemed rosy.

Dudley Wood was and is a great raconteur and bestrode the rugby stage as Committee man and Secretary. He was a natural on his feet communicating his wit and charm to the rugby clubs up and down the country. His more serious message was that the game must remain amateur – the players should not be paid. The game's heart and soul was at stake; its ethos, its teamwork, voluntary and unpaid, the game was recreational and was designed for the enthusiastic amateur and the gifted sportsman.

Dudley Wood came into the Secretary's job at the RFU in 1986, having been one of the Surrey representatives on the Committee.

He retired from his career at ICI to take on the role and seemed ideally suited, having gained experience at senior and junior club, as well as county, level while playing and in administration. He gained a Blue at

Oxford, and played for various clubs, including Waterloo, Bedford, Rosslyn Park and Streatham Croydon. He served on the Surrey County Committee, at various times being Honorary Secretary, Team Secretary and President. He was 55 years old, an accomplised speaker and an excellent communicator, and was, compared with the previous incumbents, seen as a breath of fresh air for the game, especially as he carried with him some much needed commercial experience. He handled the media well, apart from one or two hiccups, and steered England through a period – certainly the first half of the '90s – when they were successful on the field and the rebuilding of Twickenham was in full swing.

Dudley was like a piece of Blackpool rock – break him in half and the word 'amateurism' would be seen running through him. He believed in it, he felt it was right for rugby and fought as hard as anyone to protect it. In the mid-1990s, just before he retired, a lot of the press started to see him as an anachronism, the players saw him as a barrier in the way of progress and the Committee was waiting for Dudley to come out with a plan that would please everyone but keep the game as it was.

In fact, Dudley had no such plan and walked away in retirement, leaving Hallett to face the music with no magic formula. To be fair, Dudley could not have provided any magic formula, but he was quite capable of having a plan in the safe at Twickenham for what should happen when the game went open in the hope that no one ever had to open the safe. The RFU did not have that plan and, no doubt, suffered in subsequent years for the lack of it.

It didn't take too long for the antipathy felt towards Dudley Wood by the players to build up to talk and action ... even revolution. In the early 1990s during the 'Run with the Ball' campaign, he had told a would-be agent (Dudley loathed agents) at Parallel Media that he wasn't fit to cut his toenails. Brian Moore, who had his own style of charm, burned Dudley with a stream of vitriol and locked eyeballs that left no doubt as to his parentage and what he could do with his toes. Michael Herd of the *Evening Standard* described Dudley Wood at the time as King Canute dressed in the altogether holding back the tidal wave of professionalism, with the players riding the surf ... Herd's vision was becoming reality.

In June 1995, Tony Hallett, as Secretary-Designate, went with Dudley Wood to see the former President and Treasurer, Sandy Sanders, at his lovely place at Pinmill, near Ipswich in Suffolk. Both heard out Hallett's case of a change to the way in which the playing side could be rewarded. There was a blatant breaking of the rules across the Southern hemisphere which, because of differing commercial and rival sporting pressures, were raising the professional ante. In the senior game in England, 'shamateurism' was rife. The French had made it clear that a player had to be paid to be an amateur, and Wales had been practising all kinds of 'payment' deals for years. It was a mess and it would be better to take the traditional leading role and join the vanguard, so as to influence direction, argued Hallett, than to remain an ostrich.

The patient listening was at an end – never had so

much heresy been uttered by an RFU Secretary (albeit Designate). Because burglary is rife, you don't legalise it. In any case, if you are tempted, who is going to pay for it? The official line was restated – there was simply no practical case to ruin 'our game' with money talk.

A couple of weeks later, Tony Hallett, now the new Secretary, discussed with Peter Bromage, now the newly elected Chairman, how they should work together. There was mutual trust and respect for one another's strengths and acknowledgement of weaknesses. They had a simple motto during the redevelopment of Twickenham – Hallett would build it to time and Bromage would pay for it on time. 'Peter was in such ebullient form, he was almost hyperactive with optimism and plans for the future. There was nothing insurmountable,' commented Hallett.

The following morning, the news hit Hallett's desk with a sickening thud ... Peter Bromage had had a massive heart-attack and had died overnight. With his early and untimely death, the RFU, and rugby in general, lost its brightest jewel in their management crown. The RFU had no Chairman, a new Secretary and a President living in Cornwall. The professional game was about to happen. These events combined to create a period of confusion and intrigue and so much scrambling within the game that it was surely the most unhappy period in the RFU's history. With the death of Bromage, Bill Bishop, the incoming President at the July 1995 AGM, took on the role of Chairman as well as President for an interim period.

The RFU was without a permanent Chairman so they had to go through the democratic process of choosing one. Two senior Committee men on the Executive, John Jeavons-Fellows and Robert Horner, contested the vacant position, with Jeavons-Fellows narrowly beating Horner in a vote among their peers on the Executive Committee. This vote was endorsed by the full Committee and, everybody thought, based on the Queensbury Rules that the RFU had always worked by, it was assumed that it would just be a matter of going to the Special EGM in January 1996 to obtain ratification from the membership as a whole.

But the RFU was surprised when Cliff Brittle, backed by ex-President Ian Beer, put his name forward as an alternative candidate. Brittle had already been decisively beaten by Peter Bromage in a Committee vote when Bromage was appointed.

It is true to say that the Committee did not take his candidature very seriously. Always in the past, the membership had accepted what the Committee recommended. But, this time, it was different. Brittle and his supporters decided to canvas for votes. Campaigning for votes from the membership? The RFU was in turmoil ... it's unseemly ... beneath us ... whatever will they think of next?

Brittle had a manifesto, a team of supporters and, more importantly, he targeted the grass-roots of the game, the junior clubs, offering himself as their saviour in this new world of professional rugby. He positioned himself as anti-establishment, anti-senior clubs, anti-anyone who had a different opinion and was prepared to voice it. However, his campaign was clever, well targeted and hit a chord with the junior clubs and a number of the county committees, who were afraid of being marginalised in the brave new world. A procedural oddity meant that an AGM or equivalent had to be called to elect the Executive Chairman. So a Special Meeting was held at the NEC in Birmingham on 14 January 1996. Brittle was proposed by Ian Beer, President of the RFU in 1993/94, and seconded by Middlesex, dedicated supporter of the English Rugby Counties Association (ERCA).

On standing against Jeavons-Fellows, Brittle said, 'I feel it is my duty to do so ... I have numerous requests from all levels of the game to offer myself as a candidate.' He had campaigned on a platform of improving the status of the counties, and returning them to their former glory (a good strategy, as so many of the votes came from small clubs and counties). He had tapped into the traditions and structure which still remained the backbone of the game.

Air Chief Marshall Sir Michael Stear weighed in with 'There are elements within the game that would wish to turn the RFU into Twickenham PLC.' This was a swipe at Jeavons-Fellows, who was a brusque, opinionated Midlander who, in spite of his dozens of years of service to Stourbridge Rugby Club and North Midlands, was seen as one of the movers and shakers who pushed the game into professionalism. This all endeared Brittle to the Counties who saw him as their spokesman in the uncertain, turbulent world that was threatening the 'greatest game in the world'. It seemed to mean change, big change.

The RFU was caught holding a two-edged sword. The work of the Commission set up for the moratorium period laid down the foundations for a viable professional game. They sought to get the shop window in good order before attending to other areas but, in the process, hacked off the Counties and smaller clubs who considered they had been sidelined.

The moratorium was declared to allow a year's breathing space for all clubs to come to terms with the new rugby world and the financial implications of it. Also, the RFU set up the RFU Commission to consider the terms of engagement of the professional game, the shape of leagues, international fixture relations and English international playing structure.

Jeavons-Fellows's problem was that the Brittle camp dramatised the fight between the candidate who cared for the little man and the new breed of administrator, like Jeavons-Fellows, who was on the IRB Five Nations committee, European Rugby Cup Limited and the TV Committee, the sharp end of professionalism, which, at this stage of the fledgling professional game, was unacceptable to many of the rank-and-file members.

In September 1995, soon after the IRB had announced that the game was now 'open', Brittle made a speech to the English Rugby Counties Association (ERCA) meeting. ERCA represented the interests of the counties, which at one time basically controlled rugby in England, but the counties had been an anachronism for twenty years. In fairness, the counties had contributed to running the amateur game for many years at grass roots level and had done it very well. The main route into the England team had usually been by a player turning out for his club and his county in the county championship.

However, with the introduction of leagues in the late 1980s, and with the development of a pecking order in the ranking of the clubs irrespective of historical ties, players gravitated to the most successful clubs and the selectors could basically choose from a much more concentrated list of sides instead of having the players scattered around 27 counties. This led to a diminution of the influence and power of the counties and in 1995 they saw themselves as marginalised and unloved with the games' administrators betraying them. This was fertile ground for Brittle, and he took the opportunity at the ERCA meeting to sound the alarm bells to gathering disciples hanging on his every word. He complained that a few individuals and a few Unions had turned the game upside down. He criticised the IRB and their leadership and told the audience that he had spoken to a range of people involved in the game, all of whom questioned the wisdom of what happened in Paris. His audience of county officials saw their knight in shining armour on a white horse in front of them and they had their champion.

When it came to the Special Meeting, both candidates had a series of supporters backing them, but the vote was already won outside the hall. The Brittle group held a large number of proxy votes from the junior clubs and the Services (which added up to well over 200 votes) that did not bother to attend but that were more than happy to support the rebel candidate. The voting was 647 to 332 in favour of Brittle.

There is little doubt that John Jeavons-Fellows was let down by the Committee. They voted for him as their candidate but then sat back and failed to go out into the shires and pick up the proxy votes, not believing that there was an issue until it was too late. They were outflanked by the Brittle supporters and a number of the RFU old guard, including ex-Presidents Beer, Yarranton and Serfontein, who probably voted for Brittle as a protest vote against Jeavons-Fellows. They had never forgiven Jeavons-Fellows when he beat Danie Serfontein to the IRB job in 1994.

Cliff Brittle and his brother ran an equipment-hire business which he sold in 1987. He moved to Baldine, Isle of Man, and commuted from there to Staffordshire, whom he represented on the RFU Committee, and to London for meetings. He played for Old Longtonians, Stoke, Sale and Staffordshire between 1956 and 1972, coached Staffordshire and was a County selector for 11 years. He joined the RFU in 1989 and was on various sub-committees but did not make a big impression on his peer group. He was seen as a steady, amateur-principled blazer who had a distinctive dislike for Bromage, whom he saw as a non-rugby man, but importantly, as it turned out, he was an ally of several past Presidents.

He chaired his first Executive Committee Meeting in January 1996 and made his first mistake. He went round the table asking each member of the Committee to pledge allegiance to him and was told, in no uncertain terms,

Top: Jonny Wilkinson, the brilliant England outside half who could become the highest-paid player in the game from the various revenue sources that are available to him.

Bottom: Dudley Wood, the RFU Secretary from 1986 to 1995. He was a very accomplished secretary who changed the whole culture of the RFU during the amateur era but who fought against the move towards professionalism which caused the wrath of the players. Dudley retired less than two months before the game was declared open.

Rob Andrew, the former England outside half who has had his disagreements with the RFU during his time as Director of Rugby at Newcastle Falcons. Rob was hired by Sir John Hall immediately after the game went professional and has carried the flag for professional rugby in the north east.

Top: Nigel Wray, one of the owners who was in from the start and is still there at Saracens having poured millions into the club. He has advocated no relegation and cites the investment needed in the game and the problems of debt-ridden soccer to make his argument.

Bottom left: Brian Baister defeated Cliff Brittle to become Chairman of the Management Board in 1998 and brought some stability to the troubled waters of the RFU. However, he was defeated by Graham Cattermole in 2001, to some extent because Cattermole had the support of Fran Cotton, and Baister's colleagues on the RFU failed to pick up the proxy votes.

Bottom right: Phil Kearns, the Australian captain who came into serious conflict with the Australian officials as one of the leaders of the players in supporting WRC.

Top left: Brian Moore, one of the English players in the 1990s who knew that the game had to go professional but became more and more frustrated with the RFU's intransigence.

Top right: Francois Pinnear, the South African captain of the winning 1995 side who found it difficult to switch to coaching during his spell at Saracens. He was one of the prime movers in initially supporting WRC but when he turned his back on it this was the start of its collapse.

Bottom left: David Moffet, a professional administrator who came to the role of CEO of the Welsh RFU via similar jobs in Australia and New Zealand, as well as a short spell as head of Sport England. He orchestrated the change to regional teams in Wales and now has the little matter of a £66 million debt owed by the WRU to manage.

Bottom right: Bob Dwyer, one-time coach of the Australian national side which won the 1991 World Cup. He did not endear himself to the Australian management by his support of the WRC, but is now the coach of NSW.

Peter Wheeler, the CEO of Leicester Tigers. He sits on the RFU Management Board and has been one of the leading lights on behalf of the clubs since the advent of professionalism. He has come into conflict with the RFU on many occasions but has still remained a very influential figure at the senior end of the game.

Inset: Damian Hopley, Chief Executive of the Professional Rugby Players Association. He is a member of the Board of England Rugby and is fast becoming a very influential figure in the corridors of power, especially as he has the ear of the players.

Top: Francis Baron, CEO of the RFU. He has made sweeping changes at the RFU and as head of the professional staff at Twickenham he should be one of the RFU's representatives on the IRB but there seems to be a reluctance to appoint him.

Bottom left: Clive Woodward, manager of the very successful England side who has built round him a very professional support team. A disappointing 1999 World Cup has made him even more determined to succeed in 2003.

Bottom right: John Jeavons-Fellows (*right*)who was one of England's representatives on the Board of the IRB when the decision was made in Paris in August 1995 to repeal the amateur laws. John is pictured with Tony Hallett, Secretary of the RFU at the time (*left*) and Ray Williams (*back*) who was on the IRB representing Wales.

Chris Wright, the owner of London Wasps and head of the entertainment group Chrysalis. In from the start of professionalism in rugby, he was once also the owner of soccer side QPR, but fan hostility drove him out. Fortunately this type of supporters' behaviour has not happened in rugby

Fran Cotton, chairman of Club England and a previous manager of the successful British Lions in South Africa in 1997. At one stage he was a staunch supporter of Cliff Brittle.

that he had to earn that allegiance and, unfortunately, this set the scene for the rest of his tenure. He had a confrontational style which many of his peers found totally unacceptable. Nonetheless, the scene was set for a period of internal conflict which threatened to tear the game in England apart.

The campaign for the election of Cliff Brittle as Chairman of the Management Board spawned a movement which called itself the Reform Group. It was a contradictory name, because the reformers wanted to take the game back and pretend that professional rugby and senior clubs did not exist. The Group, along with Brittle's PR Agents, basically became his propaganda machine.

Although there was a committee democratically elected by all members, the Reform Group wanted to go back to the members to vote on a variety of issues. When Brittle continued to be totally outvoted by the Management Board and the Committee on every issue, the Reform Group saw this as undemocratic, and Brittle steadfastedly failed to view any of the votes as a defeat, preferring to turn the tables on the RFU by allegedly accusing all and sundry of misleading the membership and signing deals without his knowledge.

The Reform Group saw themselves as a progressive organisation that was going to reform the RFU but, paradoxically, they supported that old dodo, divisional rugby. In fact, most of what they said they wanted was already in place. They criticised the 60-plus members of the council for being undemocratic and canvassed for a committee of 18 members. They wanted 'power returned to the members'. They canvassed on their 'openness, honesty and integrity' banner with their President, Fran Cotton, ready to do battle against the non-supporters of Brittle.

In 1997, the Group criticised the RFU Committee for proposing an alternative candidate to Brittle for Chairmanship, in spite of the fact that Brittle had been proposed as an alternative to Jeavons-Fellows the year before. When the nominations of the officials for the 1997/98 season came before the members, Brittle had been sidelined by the RFU Committee and they had instead nominated Bob Rogers, a Sussex lawyer, who had been on the committee since 1986. Rogers was one of the candidates with Brittle when Peter Bromage overwhelmingly won the vote. When those who saw a past year of turmoil looked round for a replacement for Brittle, they were not overwhelmed by candidates. Rogers seemed a safe pair of hands and he had extensive experience of RFU activities having served on a range of sub-committees but, above all, he was seen as someone who had a chance to bring unity to the Union and not carry baggage that was blighting the game in England.

However, the Brittle bandwagon was on a roll. Through the Reform Group, Brittle's PR Company and high-profile supporters like Fran Cotton and Bill Beaumont, the RFU was attacked on almost every issue.

Cotton and Beaumont saw Rogers as being no more than representative of a small but influential group. Brittle, meanwhile, was accused of paying lip service to democracy whilst disagreeing fundamentally with many of the changes over the previous two years. Change is never easy, but it was felt that Brittle had done everything to make it impossible. The Richter Scale of accusations and counter-accusations was reaching breaking point.

The AGM was significant for the fact that Fran Cotton, one of Brittle's staunchest supporters, had just returned triumphantly from the Lions tour to South Africa. He received a standing ovation before accusing Tony Hallett and the President John Richardson of all sorts of misdemeanours, particularly sidelining Cliff Brittle. Will Carling, the ex-England captain, spoke in favour of Rogers, taking a sideways swipe at Brittle and his attempt to ingratiate himself with the England team on the only occasion they saw him. In the end, Brittle came out an easy winner at the AGM in July 1997, by 599 votes to 357, again due to the proxy votes picked up by the Brittle faithful out in the shires.

Brittle stood on the podium after the victory over Rogers and promised, 'I will not let you down.' Brittle was rumoured to have promised certain supporters key positions and, in fact, initially got certain people on to the Management Board but did not succeed in pushing through many of the promises he made. His candidature was never the choice of his peer group and so he could not get the majority to work with him.

Looking back, it is difficult to fully comprehend the scale of the internecine warfare between 1996 and 1998. Into this milieu, Brittle found a way to move the debate about how rugby should be administered to examining the true worth of England's existing BBC television contract. So began a second wave of events that would engulf rugby within the four Home Unions and divide English rugby between the conservatives (the traditionalists) and the progressives.

For the record, at every vote called by Brittle at Council and Management Board level, at every SGM he or his supporters called, and at every meeting between club and Council colleagues called or chaired by Brittle, he invariably lost. But extraordinarily, he always had a safe haven in amongst his Middlesex or Lancashire supporters.

The Reform Group gathered unto itself all the traditional causes – the would-be RFU councillors and those who had wanted to be voted on to the governing body. This episode was not helped by Brittle's sceptical attitude towards the media.

Brittle wished to restore the amateur game, to unstitch thread by thread the Paris Pronouncement. An early Brittle strategy for the game was outlined in his *Rugby Restructure 2000* in 1997, his vision of the future. Most of the Committee were unimpressed, particularly as Brittle had failed to send them copies of his own report.

The main points of the plan were as follows:

- Establish Club England, administered by a board of experts to ensure the national team's worldwide success
- Return the majority of the clubs to amateur status from National One downwards
- Create five semi-independent English provincial

    sides with Unions to administer the game at
    grass-roots level in their respective areas

- Create new business within Twickenham,
  including RFU television, catering, hospitality
  and merchandising
- Increase current annual turnover from around
  £50m to £300m over a ten-year period

Cecil Duckworth, owner of Worcester, was not convinced. 'I just find it amazing that such proposals can be put forward. You can't create professional rugby one day and then the next day try something else. To make some clubs amateur again is a restraint of trade.'

Trevor Richmond, the Chairman of the National Clubs Association, said, 'There has to be some kind of semi-professional level. It is impossible for clubs to go from an amateur environment into a professional one. The promoted clubs will be here for one season and will find it impossible to compete. The plan is not viable.'

In fairness to Brittle, a number of the points in the plan have since been adopted, but he was on a hiding to nothing when he suggested that the Committee voted for its own demise.

The irony of the situation was that the group that Brittle had fought so much against since the advent of professionalism, the senior clubs, would have been ring-fenced, although the number would have been 24. He had had help from an academic, a Professor of Strategy, but in the end it was too much for the committee to absorb. It was likened to 'turkeys voting for Christmas' – no direct financial assistance for clubs at the amateur level, and the development of five English provincial Unions to administer the game at grass-roots level – and it was much too much, too soon, for a Committee that was only just acclimatising to the Paris decisions of 1995.

Brittle's reaction was to go on the attack. His *coup de grace* was that he brought Fran Cotton into the battle as Chairman of the Reform Group through his Lancashire connections. In due course he managed to get his teeth into the television rights contract.

Many felt that, when England decided to negotiate its own TV rights in 1995, this was the first time anyone had thought about it. But, almost a decade earlier, Albert Agar, one of the RFU's representatives on the IRB, announced to the RFU Committee that a new TV deal had been approved. The BBC would pay £1m over three years and all four Home Unions were to divide the money equally. So, in effect, England received £55,000 per game.

John Burgess, who was to become President of the Union in 1987/88, objected to the split of monies, citing the immense size of England, and its number of clubs and players. Nothing happened. But the issue did not go away and, in November 1993, Dudley Wood wrote to Bob Weighill, Honorary Secretary of the Home Union Committee, voicing concern about the amount the RFU received from the TV contract compared with what Wood described as the 'true worth of televised coverage of rugby in this country'. He pointed out that 'England's rugby is valued, for television purposes, at more than 50 per cent of the total Home Unions' contract. It has a duty to its constituent bodies and to its member clubs, of whom there are more than 2,000, to do the best deal it can.'

He maintained that, when the RFU initiated a new and separate deal for overseas sales, the amount paid jumped from £11,250 per Union in 1987/88 to £334,109 in 1992/93 for the RFU, and £176,666 apiece for the other three Unions. Wood suggested that, in future, the RFU receive 31 per cent of the income with the rest being divided amongst the rest. This was turned down flat by the other Unions.

There were other occasions when the intention was put forward for England to negotiate its own rights, but not enough of the Committee was prepared to bite the bullet. Yet the sports budget allocated by the UK Government, largely through UK Sport to Scotland, Wales, Northern Ireland and England, has always been allocated on the basis of population rather than need or social indices or results. So, the fact that the other Unions feigned indignation does not really wash.

The minutes of the Five Nations Committee of 12 December 1995 stated, 'It was the RFU's view that they should receive a larger share for any new contract monies than the other Unions.' They had consistently opposed a three-year deal but were outvoted and had to then decide whether they should proceed with independent TV negotiations. Interestingly, the National Lottery distribution to respective Sports Councils stands at 83.3 per cent to England and Wales, 8.9 per cent to Scotland, and 2.8 per cent to Northern Ireland. Proof, if it was ever needed, of the RFU's strong case.

David Robinson, as Chairman of the Television Working Party, wrote to the Committee on 23 May 1996: 'Following a presentation to the RFU Committee on broadcasting television rights by John Jeavons-Fellows on Friday, 12 April 1996, it was resolved that the RFU would negotiate its own television rights.' Robinson proposed that the RFU must act quickly if it was to capitalise on the decisions taken to maximise its television and sponsorship rights. The vote, incidentally, to negotiate its own rights was carried by 34 votes to 7.

On the question of whether there might be serious repercussions for England, or retaliatory action taken by the other Home Unions, Jeavons-Fellows, having sought legal advice, reported that 'there is no legal reason to prevent the RFU from entering into separate TV negotiations and the other Unions would be acting contrary to both English and European law if they attempted to exclude the RFU from the Five Nations Championship ...'

In April 1996 the RFU agreed a new TV contract with Sky for the sum of £87.5 million over five years, £22.5 million of which was designated for the senior clubs. The other Unions were offered deals by Sky but rejected them out of hand.

In July the Five Nations Chairman, Tom Kiernan, announced that England had been expelled from the tournament and a protocol had been signed by the other four nations for a new tournament to be established on a home-and-away basis. In September a meeting in Bristol went long into the night but finally a deal was brokered whereby England kept their home internationals on Sky but would make a contribution into the Five Nations pot. An accord was signed by the nations attending the meeting which did not include France. England agreed not to negotiate separately again when the Sky contract ended in June 2002. In February 1997, Wales, Scotland and Ireland agreed a £40 million three-year deal with the BBC.

Away from the TV rights issue, as far as the ongoing stewardship of the RFU was concerned, the cracks grew ever wider after Brittle's appointment ... particularly between him and the Secretary at the time, Tony Hallett.

There had been an internal inquiry, initiated by Brittle, into the actions of Hallett by a high-profile group headed by Sir Patrick Lowry and including Sir Ian (now Lord) McLaurin. They found nothing of substance to level against Hallett.

However, Hallett realised quickly that there was no way in which he and Brittle could work together, and decided to fall on his sword, saying, 'Today, as I leave Twickenham for the final time as its senior executive, will be one of the saddest days I have known. The place is in my blood and I am proud of what has been achieved as the leader of one of the best sports governing bodies in the world. But there is simply no other way ... another [Brittle] would prefer to do the leading and he believes his recent re-election allows him that right. Whether he is right or wrong, history will decide. For my part, I simply cannot allow the country and the game I love to be torn apart, nor can I subject my colleagues in the RFU and the game at large to further painful bloodletting and internecine warfare. The only way is for me to resign and give Cliff Brittle the baton he craves.'

Brittle lasted another year and presided over a very troubled period in English rugby history. Open warfare broke out, the game seemed to lose its way and even Vernon Pugh opined that it had fared better with Hallett.

The RFU hierarchy had grown reminiscent of the political scene at Westminster, rather than the governing body of a national sport. Articles appeared in the *Daily Telegraph* on 26 April 1997, prior to the AGM, accusing Tony Hallett, in particular, but also Bill Bishop, of misleading the previous AGM in 1996. John Richardson, the President voted in at the 1996 AGM, came into the position hoping to build bridges and re-establish creditability at the RFU. By his own admission, he failed miserably and so, reluctantly, decided to ask one of the senior Committee men, Roy Manock, a lawyer from Yorkshire, to investigate the truth of the allegations contained in the article. In essence, the three allegations were:

- That Tony Hallett misled the AGM of the RFU by stating that he had the right to veto over pay-per-view when he did not
- That Tony Hallett tampered with the minutes of the RFU Executive and the RFU Committee
- That the RFU leadership knew of the RFU's expulsion from the Five Nations Tournament,

yet failed to disclose this to the AGM of the RFU
which took place on 12 July 1996

Manock found no evidence of any misdemeanours in any
of the allegations.

This did not come as a surprise to the vast majority of
the Committee, but Brittle would not accept Manock's
findings and basically dismissed Manock's report as of
no importance. John Richardson, the President, blew not
only a valve but a whole gasket. A very mild-mannered
man, who did not like confrontation, had had enough.
He wrote to the full Committee from Argentina where he
was touring with the England team, criticising Brittle
and the way he had conducted business in secret in a
number of areas.

John Richardson represented Warwickshire on the RFU
Committee for over 20 years. He was another lawyer
(easily the most common area of expertise on the
Committee) whose wife was very successful in exhibiting
sheep at various shows from their farm in Warwickshire.

Richardson was a quiet, unostentatious individual who
preferred the olive branch to the sword – consensus over
conflict. When he took over from Bill Bishop, he was
determined to bring unity to the game. But even
Richardson found it impossible to unite the various
sections of the game and, although he saw a sort of truce
break out between the clubs and the RFU with the
Leicester Agreement, which he had worked so hard to
achieve, he left office a sad man, realising that he'd never
managed to achieve his aims, and handed over to Peter

Brook, who was faced with trying to sort out more potentially explosive issues than the UN.

The Leicester Agreement was basically an agreement between the clubs and the RFU whereby the RFU took over EPRUC and its debts of £1.5 million and set up a joint body called England Rugby Partnership (ERP) to run the professional game.

Brook, elected to the Presidency in July 1997, had plenty of experience of making split-second decisions and being unpopular if one group did not agree with his decision. He was an international rugby referee and had made plenty of difficult decisions in his career.

However, little did he realise when he became President of the Union in 1997 that he was going to be confronted with some of the most unpleasant and acrimonious situations that anyone could imagine.

Brook was a genial person who had Yorkshire grit in his veins and built himself a sound reputation with the international rugby community while on the IRB. He was present in Paris when the decision to go open was taken and he had a very strong hand in choosing the international referees to officiate in an increasing number of international matches. His life as President was no easier than his two predecessors and, in many ways, because the attacks on him were very personal, he had to endure a year of unrelenting struggle.

Having been appointed to what he believed would be a fulfilling, challenging and thoroughly enjoyable role, Peter Brook was beside himself. He had Brittle and Graham Cattermole, Chairman of Finance and an ally of Brittle, stressing that they lacked confidence in him. He had Brittle, Cotton and Cattermole yapping like bull terriers at his heels wanting Jeavons-Fellows to resign. He felt besieged, pressured and threatened. He certainly did not sign up for the President's role to have to endure this.

Unfortunately, within a couple of years of retiring from the presidency he was diagnosed with cancer and died in 2000. What effects the traumas of his year at the helm had had on his health no one will really know.

Previously, whilst still President, John Richardson had lost patience with the feuding around him, and believed that the only way he could bring matters out into the open was to have a proper judicial inquiry under a High Court Judge, His Honour Judge Gerald Butler QC.

Butler reported in October, approximately five months after having been given the brief. He produced a 63-page document, which turned out to be very thorough. A good thing, too, as it was reputed to have cost a six-figure sum. But apart from being examined by a select few, the report was not released for public consumption. Considering there were highly personal charges and counter-charges that questioned the integrity of Hallett and Bishop, in particular, the President should have at least publicly cleared those who were innocent of any misdemeanours.

Butler cleared Hallett on all the accusations made against him, and similarly Bill Bishop. Neither received an apology privately, nor in public, from Brittle. Both had left their positions by the time the report was issued but, in his postscript, the Judge made a telling statement:

The professional era both needs and deserves professional management and administration. Honorary officials, or to put it more bluntly, amateurs, are no longer suitable for the post. It concerns me equally that he is elected by the membership. I would suggest that members are simply not in a position to properly assess the suitability of a candidate for the post. I believe that, if rugby is to continue to thrive at every level, and to expand further, it is the professional game that must take the lead.

And so say all of us.

On the question of the ongoing feud between Hallett and Brittle, the Judge felt that both had acted as though they should be the person who should be responsible for the day-to-day business of the RFU and they both could not be in charge. However, he had no doubt that matters were not helped by what seemed to be Brittle's 'unshakeable belief that he was always right'.

He even quoted Oliver Cromwell from a letter sent to the General Assembly of the Church of Scotland in 1650. 'I beseech you in the bowels of Christ, think it possible you may be mistaken.'

Despite these sincere and expensive attempts to purge the RFU of incessant infighting, the feuds and arguments in 1997 did not abate.

Rob Andrew launched a blistering attack on the RFU in August 1997 accusing them of attempting to destabilise the club game by approaching certain players regarding the signing of contracts with the RFU when their contracts expired.

'These approaches are totally underhand. They [the RFU] are under a delusion that England can have a similar set-up in New Zealand and South Africa where the Union is dominant and where the prime feeder to the national team is through the provinces. Cliff Brittle and Fran Cotton have come to power on a ticket of openness and honesty. It's time to deliver on it. The rugby public should know what's going on. The club owners had the courage to invest in the game. They have done more for the game in 12 months than the game has done for itself in the previous 100 years, the RFU should stop being paranoid.'

Policy-making, as has been shown, was often impossible to achieve, with so many diverse opinions and interests hanging on every decision. But, occasionally, strategies found a consensus.

During the wash-up of the National Playing Committee following the Rugby World Cup in 1995, in which Jonah Lomu ran all over the England in the semi-final, Don Rutherford, the Technical Director, reported that Jason Leonard had exclaimed, 'We'll never beat the buggers from the Southern hemisphere until we play them home and away every year.'

From this one statement, a policy was born, and over the next six months or so, the task fell to John Jeavons-Fellows to meet with, speak to or correspond with his IRB SANZAR representatives.

John Jeavons-Fellows had joined the RFU Committee in

1983. He was elected as one of the RFU's IRB reps in 1994. He enjoyed the position and could never be described as a shrinking violet. He made his views known and, although he often gave the impression of coming from the Sydney Charm School, he certainly built up a strong relationship with the Southern hemisphere delegates. Thanks to his efforts, a programme of games was formulated and reported to the National Playing Committee.

It is because of moves like this, and more of a willingness among those in power at the RFU to listen to those at the sharp end of the game, that England is currently enjoying a period of dominance on the field, seeing them in the summer of 2003 beating both New Zealand and Australia in their own back yards.

Although the move to a full-time professional sport did not please a large group of rugby followers in the UK, that could not be said for the players. England has benefited considerably from the game becoming full-time for the élite English-qualified professional players. They are fitter, stronger, more skilful, more determined and results-orientated than any other players before them. They live the lives of professional sportsmen and the results over the last 12 months have placed England as favourites for the World Cup in 2003, although New Zealand cannot be ruled out as the team to beat. In the 15 months to June 2003, England had 13 straight wins and a Six Nations Grand Slam, plus double wins against both New Zealand and Australia with the first win in Oz by any England side after ten previous attempts.

The results were stunning:

2002

March 23	beat Wales 50-10
April 7	beat Italy 45-9
June 22	beat Argentina 26-18
Nov 9	beat New Zealand 31-28
Nov 16	beat Australia 32-31
Nov 23	beat South Africa 53-3

2003

Feb 15	beat France 25-17
Feb 22	beat Wales 26-9
March 9	beat Italy 40-5
March 22	beat Scotland 40-9
March 30	beat Ireland 42-6
June 14	beat New Zealand 15-13
June 21	beat Australia 25-14

At the top level in any sport, the difference between winning and losing can be so small. A putt lipping the hole, a volley hitting the line, a goalpost saving the keeper or a conversion drifting wide at the last second all make winners and losers on the day. But the best sides do not rely on these tiny margins and 'fate'. They have prepared so assiduously that even bad luck does not enter into their vocabulary. They have thought of everything down to the smallest detail, so they win whatever the circumstances.

The Australian cricket side has 'winners' written all over

them, and now so do the England rugby side. Under Clive Woodward, nothing is left to chance. Colin Herridge wrote earlier that he had to pay his fare to South Africa when he was asked to travel with the team in 1994 as Media Liaison Officer. That was only nine years ago. Now, the official accompanying party can be around 15-strong and can include a chef, a video analyst expert, two masseurs, two physios and a line-out expert. When England played Ireland for the Six Nations decider in April 2003, they had their usual mode of transport, the team coach and driver, shipped to Dublin to keep them as close as possible to their familiar surroundings.

Nothing is left to chance. The players are treated to the best in every possible way from hotels and meals to training facilities, travel, analysis, and so on. Compared with what the two previous managers Geoff Cooke and Jack Rowell had to spend, it is light years away, but it has brought unknown success to English rugby. It has given the game its highest profile ever (the tabloids are now devoting at least three pages to England games), and there is a logical reason for saying that, with the largest player pool in the world and the largest budget to spend, England could remain the outstanding side for years to come.

But sport is unpredictable, so it is important for all supporters of England to savour the triumphs. Whatever has happened or may happen off the field, the players have taken professional rugby on board and have never looked back, since the late Vernon Pugh QC made the historic announcement on 27 August 1995.

In December 1997, another farcical episode occurred when allegations were made against John Jeavons-Fellows by Brittle, Cotton and Cattermole. These allegations were investigated by a panel of inquiry headed by Sandy Sanders, an ex-president, which found Jeavons-Fellows had no case to answer. It all became sad and would have been considered better entertainment than a Whitehall farce if it had not been so serious for the future of the game. Michael Calvin, writing in the *Mail on Sunday* in April 1998, said, 'Debate has been reduced to the level of the schoolyard, a sad sequence of slur, scorn and scare story. The private thuggery of the scrum has nothing against the murky rituals of committee room character assassinations.'

In May 1998, in a move to draw a line under past differences and vested interests, and as a genuine attempt to move the game forward, negotiating teams were set up to formulate an agreement between the RFU, English First Division Rugby Limited (EFDR), English Second Division Rugby Limited (ESDR) and the English Rugby Partnership (ERP). This became known as the Mayfair Agreement.

The principles of the Agreement stipulated that the RFU and the clubs would look after their own parts of the game, player contracts and structure of the season.

The agreement was subject to review at the end of season 2004/5. Graham Smith, a past supporter of Brittle and Chairman of the negotiating team, was peeved at Brittle's opposition to the Agreement in the face of overwhelming support by the Management Board and

Council, and he went into print making his points very clearly. Brittle had lost another ally.

By the spring of 1998, Brittle faced another rival for the position of Chairman of the Management Board, Brian Baister. Baister was a retired senior police officer who came on to the RFU Committee in the mid-'90s as one of the National Club members. Brittle had the support of Fran Cotton and the Reform Group but, more significantly, Committee members who previously had been strong allies of Brittle changed sides. Graham Smith, who had been a key speaker on behalf of Brittle, wrote, 'I believe if we are to have any chance of taking advantage of the opportunity to develop a new spirit of partnership and go forward together for the good of England, our Premier Clubs and the whole game, we should not support Cliff Brittle's attempt to be re-elected. I urge you to give Brian Baister your support.'

The membership in the end voted to end Brittle's reign as head of the RFU. Baister won the vote and another chapter in the saga of the Chairman's role of the RFU was to begin.

When Brittle was defeated by Brian Baister, the Reform Group went into hibernation but came back with a vengeance in January 1999. Having helped to put Brittle into power in 1996, they had the chance to support the Chairman of the Management Board to put in place all the changes they wanted; to follow their openness, honesty and integrity line, and bring the game together if they felt that it was inexorably drifting apart.

Fran Cotton, who was still at the time President of the

Reform Group, and also a member of the Management Board, dived in and threatened a vote of no confidence in the Management Board.

As Paul Ackford, writing in the *Sunday Telegraph*, said at the time, 'Cotton has no truck with those who believe that it is time to move forward and that the Reform Group are simply rehashing old arguments which should have been laid to rest long ago.'

The Reform Group obtained the required number of signatures to call a Special Meeting. But this time the RFU were ready. Bill Beaumont was used as a charm offensive, including recording a hotline message on the telephone. The RFU rejected the Reform Group resolutions which Beaumont said would make the game ungovernable and create chaos.

At last, the RFU had got the message. 'A vote in favour of any of the resolutions is not a vote for democracy, nor is it a vote for openness, honesty and integrity. It is a vote for confusion, a vote which will endanger the prosperity of the game,' ran the message on the hotline.

The irony of the situation was that Beaumont was voting against his own county, Lancashire, who backed the meeting. The RFU got its act together and collected the proxy votes, but a great deal of money was spent. The SGM was justified by Martyn Thomas, Chairman of the Reform Group. 'If nothing else, then the SGM will have acted as a warning shot across the RFU's bows.'

But the *Sunday Times* was able to expose the tactics of the Reform Group by showing that, where 200 clubs had supposedly called for the SGM, it was, in fact, a single individual or a small group in a club that had signed, and most of the members knew nothing about it.

In the end, the Reform Group, pilloried by the media for being a complete waste of time, lost out heavily to the RFU. Even Fran Cotton distanced himself from what he described as the 'extreme voices' in the Reform Group.

Brian Baister served as Chairman of the RFU for three years until 2001, and he would have liked to have been re-elected for a further period. The dramas and bloodletting at the Union had, by comparison with the period up to 1998, subsided, and Baister could point to a number of notable successes. These included the appointment of a Chief Executive, the significant improvement of finances and community rugby becoming a priority. There were also signs that the relationship between the Premier clubs and the RFU was improving.

Baister could also point to the fact that, over a pint at a Glasgow pub, he and the chairman of the Six Nations, Alan Hosie, struck an agreement whereby England should abide by the accord signed in 1996 and would not be threatened with dismissal from the championship for a second time.

But that old Achilles heel surfaced again – woe betide anyone who supposedly ignored or downgraded the grass-roots of the game.

Brittle had won two elections based on positioning himself as champion of the small club. Baister, who came from a junior club himself, did not see himself as ignoring them but made the mistake of not stroking enough egos at that level. His rival for the post, though, Graham Cattermole, who had been a strong Brittle supporter, saw his opportunity. He wrote in his manifesto: 'The development of the game at grass-roots in England has been neglected and the problems of the clubs below the Premiership have escalated ... action has been slow and is currently having little effect. I will take the lead in addressing these problems.'

This was music to the ears of those clubs that were suffering from a lack of administrators, escalating expenses and a dwindling number of players and teams. It was a chance to man the barricades and, with Fran Cotton leading the charge for Cattermole, he defeated Baister at the July 2001 AGM.

Graham Cattermole came on to the RFU Committee in 1996 as one of the Middlesex representatives. He was one of the staunchest supporters of Brittle and an activist for Middlesex with the Reform Group. A diehard county man he saw the opportunity to challenge Brian Baister for the role of Chairman of the Management Board in 2001 and, like Brittle, appealed to the grass-roots of the game

He had powerful supporters, including Fran Cotton, and won the vote. He has been the Chairman for two years and he chairs the meetings without fuss. He is still ambitious and plays the political game very well, no doubt seeing a role for himself on the international scene.

The defeat was all the more galling for Baister because he was basically let down by his own peer group, as had happened with Jeavons-Fellows back in 1996. His Council peers forgot that contested positions were only won by proxy votes. Although the majority of them were happy to see Baister continue, they failed to go out into their constituencies and tell the voters, as well as picking up the proxies. The Reform Group rallied and played their part in the shires so, in spite of strong support from the outgoing President Budge Rogers, Baister became another ex-something-or-other.

Subsequently, the most significant event in the summer of 2001 was the signing of an agreement between the Premier clubs and the RFU. The agreement basically outlined the running of international and Premiership rugby in England. It consisted of five nominees from the RFU and five from Premier Rugby, among whose number included the Professional Rugby Players' Association Chief Executive Damian Hopley.

During the first 18 months of the new era of understanding and reconciliation between the clubs, the players and the RFU, there has been an uneasy relationship over several issues, not least the release of players for England training, the amount of days required for training by the England team manager and payment of money to clubs from the RFU.

The clubs have an agreement with the England management about the number of days that the players are released for international training. Some clubs that provide a half-dozen or more players to the training sessions have complained that the number of days has been creeping up, and it affects their own preparations for upcoming League or Cup games. Leicester, in particular, who had a moderate season by their own standards in 2002/03, were unhappy about what they saw as the constant loss of players to the detriment of their own preparations.

There is a delicate balance between England's requirements and keeping the club coaches on side. The coaches see their own careers tied closely with the success or otherwise of their club so they are sensitive to losing players too regularly.

The agreement signed by the RFU and the clubs specifically covered the release of players so the England management feel within their rights to expect attendance at all training sessions by all those invited.

The RFU insists on promotions and regulation; Premier club owners insist that they cannot invest in a fledging professional sport if they do not have security of tenure, having already put £150m into professional club rugby.

This has become a contentious issue and a panel of three members representing Premier Rugby (PRL) and three from the first division (FDR) met in June 2003 under the chairmanship of Francis Baron, CEO of the RFU. A decision was made, by four votes to three, that automatic promotion and relegation would continue, the casting vote going to Francis Baron with the clubs at a three-all stalemate.

The Premier clubs expressed 'extreme disappointment' at the outcome: 'Premier Rugby believes that this decision is not in the interests of the professional game in England and will actually have a considerable, damaging effect on the agreed objectives of the England national team and 12 professional clubs, as it does not encourage nor enable the professional clubs to plan beyond 12 months in any aspect of their business ... and it is likely to have a damaging effect on England's chances of winning the Rugby World Cup in 2007.

'Premier Rugby feels the decision is a massive blow to the future of the professional game in this country and that, once again, English sport has been let down by not ensuring it has the right tools to perform at the highest level on the world stage.'

The owners do not feel that they have been given credit for their contribution to the England side. They know that the RFU could not have afforded to finance the professional game, and they have contributed enormously by providing outstanding players with the requisite professional skills and experience.

Now that they have lost their battle over promotion and relegation, it is a moot point as to whether the intention to have more English-qualified players will come to fruition when push comes to shove. Will most teams follow Newcastle's example and bring in foreign players when the going gets tough, and the danger of relegation becomes more of a priority for them than developing talented English-qualified international players? A sorry consequence of the reality that those who pay the piper ...

There seems to be little hope of this situation being turned around in the foreseeable future. A further decline in the relationship between the clubs and the RFU therefore seems inevitable.

As far as the general state of the RFU structure is concerned, change is in the air. The RFU's Council cannot stay the way it is. Even a traditionalist such as Budge Rogers, President of the RFU in 2000/01, realised that the administrative structure of the game had to change. 'The constitution which allows the game to be run by the junior elements of the game just does not work.'

The old committee structure was, in the main, based on representatives from constituent bodies (i.e. the counties) with additional representatives from the Services, Oxbridge, other universities and schools. The President and the officers were the senior officials who, together with the Executive Committee, were the principal group that ran the game. The Committee, which met around six times a year, generally in the Hilton Hotel, Park Lane, consisted of more than 55 which, together with the professional staff, involved a meeting of around 60 people.

It was like any other amateur committee around the world in any sport. A range of members whose individual contribution varied enormously. It came to decisions based on a majority vote and, because of the make-up of the Committee, some members were mandated by their constituent bodies, while others were able to vote as they thought fit. It was all very much like the political parties in the House of Commons.

In many ways, it did not matter in the amateur days that the talking shop saw itself as the guardian of the game, and as long as it ran the game in a benevolent but autocratic style, the clubs, in the main, just got on with their own affairs but longed for a successful England side which Geoff Cooke produced in the first half of the 1990s. Everything in the Committee garden was blooming. Dudley Wood was the ideal spokesman for the amateur game and was intellectually streets ahead of many of his colleagues – 'follow the leader' was the simplest and most non-confrontational thing to do.

The severe discontent of the players was rationalised by categorising them as greedy, money-seeking, 'here today, gone tomorrow' upstarts trying to sabotage the game and, besides, if you played all your rugby for the Old Rubberduckians' 3rd XV and had never been paid a penny, why should the likes of Carling, Moore, Guscott et al receive anything for playing 'the greatest team game in the world', as most Committee men were fond of saying to rapturous applause.

However, to suddenly find that a committee of 60 or so had the responsibility to administer a professional game, which most of them did not want and could not understand, was bound to lead to problems. Unfortunately, the problem was way beyond comprehension for most of the members and it developed into a monumental row between warring groups within the RFU, the clubs, the counties, the four Home Unions, the IRB and anyone else who wanted a scrap, with the players caught in the middle but giving their twopenny worth. The *modus operandi* had to change but, in the meantime, World War III erupted in rugby circles.

Changes were made and the number of committees has decreased dramatically, with only committees to oversee England rugby (Club England), Finance and Funding, Governance, Community and Development, and six sub-committees.

The Management Board, comprising 13 members, meeting ten times a year (with extra meetings if required), has a mixture of professionals and council members. The Council only meets three or four times a year and much of the work previously handled by sub-committees is now done by the professionals. When Francis Baron joined as Chief Executive, he oversaw a major cull of the staff, but, four years on, the numbers have crept up and there are now over 200 on the payroll.

The issue is whether or not the Constitution should be changed. The membership voting for the Chairman is out of date but, as we have seen, there would be an uprising if the RFU attempted to change the voting.

There is the question of whether the professional game should be completely divorced from the amateur game, with two separate groups, and also the problem of funding for the future. The RFU has laid out its plans but there are major issues of how clubs at various levels will react as the RFU brings in more money from increased revenue at Twickenham and sponsorship.

We favour a small, overarching executive of eight led by the Chief Executive, with three main committees beneath that, of equal status – one for the international game, one for the professional clubs and one for the amateur clubs.

Before this can happen, though, there needs to be a closer relationship between the professional clubs and the RFU

Committee men. There are a number of the RFU Council, as well as some professional administrators, who are uncomfortable with the owners. It is hard to gauge whether this is because all the owners are rich, opinionated, driven individuals, who do not suffer fools gladly and have no truck with those still reminiscing about the amateur days, or whether there is a genuine belief that they want to control the international game. You can count on the fingers of one hand (or almost one finger) the number of the Council who have any real association with a Premiership club (Peter Wheeler, the CEO of Leicester, being the most obvious exception) so, to be kind, perhaps much of the distrust is because nobody has run a professional sports business using their own money.

The owners are getting frustrated, which plays into the hands of those who did not want the owners in the first place, who wanted the RFU to contract the players anyway, and who would still like to see six regional sides playing under the entire control of the RFU. It would only take three or four of the owners to up sticks, and the anti-owner group would get their wish. Where the money would come from to pay some 200 players, and to fund the administrative and coaching structure, ground hire, marketing and getting the public to watch amorphous groups playing in atmosphere-less stadiums is a good question. If all the RFU's resources went into this pot, would the rest of the game see any money cascading down to the grass-roots, because one estimate is that running a regional competition as the top tier below the national team would cost in the region of £40m–£50m per year?

However, the desire is there and the liaison between the Premier clubs and the RFU is starting to go downhill after the initial honeymoon period.

It's much worse if you are Wales or Scotland. The GDP of these countries is not yet sufficient for them to be able to afford to run sport on the scale that England does, especially when the sport concerned is rugby union. If England chooses to go the way of its cousin, English soccer (which pulled out of the Home International series), then this will only exacerbate the issue. In a sense, therefore, the three funding agencies for smaller professional rugby-playing countries must be the IRB, governments and their own Rugby Unions. Given that this isn't rocket science, it again calls into question as to why these lesser-playing countries voted for France and not England for RWC2007. In the short term, they have cut off their noses to spite their faces; in the longer term, they might just have signed their own death warrants.

6

ON THE UP DOWN UNDER

In rugby union history, Australia has had to suffer the tag of the 'nearly nation' for much longer than was ever necessary. The Aussies quite often beat the four Home Unions on tours to the UK though they had to wait until 1984 for a grand slam of wins. In Australia, few countries came away with victories. But across the water, the always-legendary All Blacks held sway well beyond their sell-by date.

The issue for the Australian Rugby Union Board was how were they to keep growing the game at home whilst achieving greatness at international level. Coming off the back of the 1984 Grand Slam, many pundits thought Australia had a strong chance to win the inaugural Rugby World Cup in 1987, but it wasn't to be.

In Australia, rugby union frequently lags behind League, Aussie Rules and soccer in the media, especially when it comes to television schedules. If the Australians were to maintain their position on the world stage, they would have to be nimble but, above all else, they had to be first. 'First to what?' you may ask; first to take the game open.

Australia always had a different problem from all the other major rugby-playing countries, except, to a much lesser extent, Wales. They constantly lost players to rugby league. Union was considered the 'rah rah' game played by the middle-class, whereas professional rugby league accommodated the working-class sportsman. League was the dominant rugby game with large crowds, good stadia, wealthy sponsors and extensive media coverage, albeit exclusively in the two States, Queensland and New South Wales. Australia were also the World Champions in League and had most of the best rugby players in the world in either code.

Union was practically an academy for the League game, whereby it was the ambition of many a player to reach a certain standard in Union (generally State or international status) and hope to be offered terms by a leading league club. Leading club sides like Randwick in Sydney would regularly lose several players to rugby league every year where the profile was so much higher, and the best players could earn a living from becoming a professional rugby player. Although Wales lost a number of good players who went 'north', it was nothing compared with the exodus that occurred in Union in Australia.

In November 1991, following the Wallabies' victory

against England in the 1991 Rugby World Cup, R B 'Dick' McGruther wrote a briefing paper for discussion purposes for the Queensland Rugby Union (QRU) and the Australian Rugby Football Union (ARU) on the topic STRUCTURED PLAYER BENEFITS — APPEARANCES AND COMMUNICATION. The document covered 23 pages!

Dick McGruther was at the time Chairman of the QRU and a director of the ARU, as well as one of the movers and shakers in Australian rugby. Dick is a no-holds-barred, say-what-you-think Australian, who famously referred to England's visit in 1998 as a 'Tour of Hell' and the 'biggest sell-out since Gallipoli'. This was when England took a very below-strength side to Australia and got walloped in the Test by 78 points to nil.

However, Dick was also one of those far-sighted Southern hemisphere officials who realised that the game was moving inexorably towards professionalism, notwithstanding the fact that there was no desire on behalf of the IRB to do much except contemplate its growing navel. Australia was haemorrhaging players on a regular basis to rugby league and, in order to stop the defection from becoming a mass exodus, McGruther wanted a discussion to take place on the way players could receive benefits within the IRB regulations. His view was that 'we must move more urgently to assess the situation and to formulate any changes, particularly if we wish to shape and control those changes. There are sufficient grounds for speculation out there now which will only be exasperated after players return from the World Cup.'

McGruther felt that separate financial arrangements were needed as they might apply to 'élite player retention' and 'team entitlements'. At the time, Australia was very worried about their best players switching to rugby league. They had continually lost their best players to League over the years, but they were fast becoming one of the best sides in the world having just won the 1991 World Cup in England. So they wanted to put in place financial packages which they considered to be within the IRB regulations, but which they felt would persuade their top players to stay in Union.

First of all, the ARU, in negotiations with the players, agreed to set up 'Team Entitlements' under the auspices of the Players' Promotions and Marketing Fund (PPMF). This was to raise and control funds generated from promotions and marketing activities both from within rugby and from outside sources, and which could capitalise on team profile – golf days, for example, or player appearances. It was proposed to distribute these funds equitably to team members. There was also some provision for placing the Union under some obligation to contribute to PPMF.

The Union felt the system would, from the players' perspective, offer a financial advantage, add to team harmony and co-operation and would result in more of the top players remaining loyal to the game.

From the Union point of view, it would mean that the Union could retain control of sponsorship negotiations and avoid conflict in the marketplace, and maintain and improve playing performance through player retention. The ARU realised that there were categories of 'permitted' and 'non-permitted' activity under the IRB Rules, but they concluded that there was nothing in the By-laws or Regulations which excludes the players from benefiting financially from promotional and marketing activities.

In addition to PPMF, McGruther felt that the ARU needed to consider separately the concept of 'élite player retention'. It was envisaged that there would be no more than four or five players in a squad who could be considered 'élite'. The focus would be on employment/career opportunities because there was evidence that commercial organisations, particularly those with a current association with the Union, were prepared to embrace employment situations for the élite player. McGruther, therefore, felt that an attempt should be made to structure some commercial association between employers and the Union.

From these actions, McGruther concluded that the ARU would answer the problem of losing players to League while remaining within the IRB Rules. Remember, this was in 1991, four years before the meeting in Paris, but here was a Union looking positively at ways to reward the players financially. Meanwhile, in the Northern hemisphere, the four Home Unions were looking for ways to close any loopholes that could allow players to earn money in any way from the game

McGruther made the point that the first stage of addressing the issue of financial reward, which was a battle conducted over many years, was to secure the necessary amendments to the IRB Regulations. Australia felt they had achieved this in the early part of 1991.

The second stage, the framing of local by-laws, had already commenced. But McGruther also had the foresight to realise that the players were going to secure financial benefits by some means as a result of the changes in the Regulations. 'If you accept that these points are inevitable, then the argument for rugby officials to take the initiative becomes fairly apparent.'

The discussion paper covered a whole range of issues including what was 'permitted' and 'not permitted' under IRB Regulations, the setting up of the Players' Promotions and Marketing Fund (PPMF), the control, ownership and commercial arrangements, distribution of benefits and, most importantly, élite player retention.

As McGruther concluded, 'The two concepts of Team Entitlements and Élite Player Retention undoubtedly include concepts which are unprecedented.' But he was confident that his suggestions would be adopted because he had already arranged to have various business names, including 'Wallabies Promotions and Marketing' and 'Queensland Reds Promotions and Marketing' registered. He also had prepared draft documents for Élite Player Agreements and for PPMF, as well as obtaining the opinion of a Queen's Counsel on the compliance aspects of the proposals.

This was four years before the IRB declared the game 'open'. Australia, as well as the All Blacks and Springboks, were quite justified in sensing that 'something was in the air'.

The ARU set up a Trust fund and told the players that there would be a distribution of Trust money which would depend on the number of games they played for the Wallabies, as well as their own commercial viability. The IRB became very jittery over these activities and an Australian delegation was invited to Dublin and London to discuss what they were doing.

McGruther had a quaint Aussie description for various events. The reader will remember his description of the England 'tour of hell' in 1998. He was as colourful about the reception the delegates received when they turned up at the East India Club in St James's Square, London – the traditional meeting venue for the IRB. McGruther described it as a 'Star Chamber' interrogation. The Star Chamber got its name from the old English prerogative court which flourished in the late 16th and early 17th century, a tribunal that had far-ranging authority and had the reputation of not allowing those accused any chance of redeeming themselves.

The IRB did not seem to be able to get their mind around the trust fund activity which the ARU was using to pay their players. The ARU was not prepared to see the continued exodus of players from their ranks to professional rugby league and was prepared to defend their actions whatever the IRB might say or feel.

The Australian personnel were left to wait outside the meeting room and then invited in, and had a short time to put their case before an adjournment for lunch. The IRB was getting put more and more under pressure from the Southern hemisphere and were in no position to pretend that what was happening in Australia was not happening – the writing was on the wall. The IRB had basically lost control. The Australians had set out their stall and invited the IRB to challenge what they had done as being illegal under the IRB regulations. A *laissez-faire* attitude prevailed

The IRB hadn't the guts or the inclination to either ban them or suspend the ARU Committee. Whereas the ARU understood its position and wanted to keep its players, the IRB did not.

To be frank, did the Aussies really care less any more? They had, after all, been planning something else which would give the Southern hemisphere nations a huge boost and a substantial income-generating activity to boot! South Africa, New Zealand and Australia had committed themselves to a Super 10 'provinces' or 'State' competition to start in 1993. Players were going to be away on mini tours and they would hear what each provincial club was paying in terms of expenses, which just added to the demands from them to be adequately compensated. They felt the administrators were not moving fast enough, despite their earlier initiatives. They wanted nothing more and nothing less – they wanted to be paid for playing. It was the Southern hemisphere players who kick-started the rugby revolution.

Union, Down Under, had very little to entice the good player to stay in Union, particularly if he did not have a job with good prospects or an understanding employer who let him have enough free time for training and touring. The Union officials took this as one of the occupational hazards of running the Union game, especially as they did not have any significant influence on the IRB until the late 1980s. However, the annual raiding by rugby league continued.

Super League was launched in Australia in April 1995, two months before the opening of the 1995 Rugby World Cup in South Africa. Financed by Rupert Murdoch, it was challenging the establishment of Australian rugby league and signing up as many players as it could to play in a new competition. The financial rewards were mind-boggling – players who had been paid A$150,000 were being offered A$500,000.

The top cats were offered A$800,000, with a signing-on fee of A$200,000. Rugby league had always been a thorn in the side of Union, but now it could threaten its whole existence and the State officials had to act quickly. In a joint statement, the New South Wales and Queensland Rugby Unions said, 'The rugby world has been remunerating players and coaches in various ways for a very long time ... Amateurism as a concept is outmoded and should be dispensed with in the modern game.'

They were apoplectic about what might happen to many of the stars if they were approached to sign on for the figures being handed out to League players. In fact, a number of the Wallabies were not without income from rugby. Eleven of them had been put on a payment of A$75,000 a season to ensure their endorsement of ARU sponsors and to make promotional appearances. But this was chicken feed compared to what the League boys were being offered and a number of them saw the dollar signs growing ever larger before their eyes.

The ARU had to do something, if only it was to shout out loud, 'Benefactors, where are you? Save our game!' They actually did more than that because, in late April, the CEOs of New South Wales, Queensland and the ARU, namely David Moffett, Terry Doyle and Bruce Hayman, were sitting down and hatching a plan that they would sell as 'The Perfect Rugby Product'.

Bruce Hayman sent a memo to Leo Williams and Phil Harry, Chairman and President respectively of the ARU, in April 1995, in which he referred to 'The Perfect Rugby Product'. Hayman said, 'In the wake of the Super League raid on the ARL and the subsequent speculation surrounding rugby at international and provincial level, we felt it was important to adopt immediately a co-ordinated approach by the three major Unions in respect of the entire rugby product.

'In particular, we were concerned that we were sitting on our hands waiting for organisations outside rugby to come forward with proposals for our consideration. If, on the other hand, we are to control our own destiny and manage the change effectively, it is imperative that we develop an integrated strategy involving all Unions in Australia, especially the major Unions which already have commitments to international programmes.'

He had spoken to George Verry from the NZRFU and also Edward Griffith, Chief Executive of the South African RFU. Hayman also believed that, to attract an investor/partner of their choice, they should adopt the very structured approach as outlined in the recommendations which formed the catalyst for the SANZAR agreement with News Corp in July, only three months from the date of the memo.

Necessity is the mother of invention and, if there was a necessity for Southern hemisphere rugby to produce the golden egg, this was the time. History shows they came up with the Super 12, which was an extension of the previous Super 6 and 10, and the icing on the cake, the Tri-Nations – a home-and-away Test series played between the three Southern hemisphere giants. They then had to sell this concept to one of the media moguls. At the same time, they knew Ross Turnbull had started to beat the drum extolling his World Rugby Corporation venture.

When the players left for South Africa for the start of the World Cup, not one had actually signed for Super League, but how would they react when they came home after the tournament was anyone's guess. Phil Harry, President of the ARU, let the players know that Turnbull might be touting for their business in South Africa and they should resist as the ARU had its own negotiations and would be announcing its intentions very soon.

Phil Harry had been one of the stalwarts of the Sydney University side in his playing days, but when he stopped playing he did not turn his hand to administration. He developed a successful business career while maintaining his interest in rugby and raising a family, which included his son, Richard, a strapping back-row forward.

Phil got the call to arms when New South Wales were in trouble in the late 1980s with the Concord Oval. His skill in helping out in a difficult situation propelled him into national officialdom and, when Joe French, the laconic President of the ARU, died, Phil became President in 1994, with Leo Williams as Chairman, a man who knew how to party, as befits his huge frame.

Phil continued in the post until 2000, presiding over some of the most momentous times in Wallaby rugby history, including the World Cup in Cardiff in 1999, when his son Richard, having converted to a prop, played in the winning team. Phil was at the coalface when the game was threatened by Super League, the targeting of players by the WRC, the signing of the SANZAR agreement with News Corp, and the change to an 'open' game.

An inveterate talker, he presided over the Committee changes with the advent of professionalism and knows as much as anyone about the politics of rugby.

As Phil Harry said, 'We embraced professionalism when it came because we were moving towards it anyway by 1995. We were planning to go professional and it looked as though this would happen two years after the World Cup in 1995. We had our own idea on how to do it and, when South Africa came back into the fold, we talked a lot more to New Zealand about the move to professionalism. We thought that if something did not change in a few years, we would have to make moves to what we thought was inevitable.'

In 1994, the Australians sent an emerging Wallabies

side to Zimbabwe and South Africa. Because of the threat of players switching to rugby league, all players selected for the tour were advised by Bruce Hayman, the CEO of the ARFU, that they would be required to sign an undertaking that, as members of the touring party in a development team, they would be available for selection (subject to injury) for the World Cup touring squad in 1995. The undertaking identified that if they would not be available for the World Cup, they would have to repay to the ARU the costs related to preparation and touring with the team. This was estimated to be in the order of $25,000.

At the time, Bruce heard a rumour as to the likelihood of at least one player planning to sign with rugby league on the team's return from the tour. This forced Peter Jorgensen to withdraw from the tour and he signed with League. Ironically, Jorgensen is back in Union playing for Northampton in the Premiership.

During the tour, at Victoria Falls, Phil Harry told a special players' meeting that the move to professionalism was inevitable and would occur in the near future and they would be better off to stay within rugby union than switch to League.

Australia already had major problems with the labour laws because some players who had gone to rugby league wanted to come back into Union. Bruce Hayman remembers, 'If we prevented them from coming back into rugby union, we were restricting trade and this became a major issue for us with the IRB in 1994. Virtual reality is such that eventually the word "virtual" goes and "reality" kicks in. A prominent Scottish Committee man told me that, if players wanted to be paid for playing, they should go to rugby league. The Northern hemisphere was still in the virtual reality mode, and this was the big difference. Virtual reality in the Northern hemisphere; reality in the Southern.'

Although Australia had the Wallaby Promotions and Marketing which they considered was a clear indication of their intent for the players, the advent of the World Rugby Corporation in 1995 threatened the whole hegemony of the game. It seemed as if the world of rugby was heading for a Packer-led hijacking, just as he had accomplished in cricket in the 1970s.

In 1992, Pay TV was introduced to Australia, and Murdoch and Packer knew that the way to make Pay TV work was to own sporting rights. This opened up the way for big cheques to be written out for professional sport. The ARU was aware of this. In 1991, the TV fee to the ARU was $A200,000. In 1995, the ARU contract with Channel 10 was worth $A2m. This may not appear a lot by UK standards, but it was still a considerable hike from previous contracts and rugby union executives like Ian Ferrier, the Treasurer of the NSWRFU, saw the opportunity of Pay TV. The plan was to join with South Africa and New Zealand in 1995 and design a new competition, which could then be sold to Pay TV. However, when the WRC came in, Ferrier and others realised that if they did not win the fight, then they might lose everything.

There is no doubt that, although the tentacles of the

WRC reached out to all the rugby-playing nations, the toughest battle occurred in Australia and the architect of the WRC, Ross Turnbull, has his own views as to why the WRC was needed and why, ultimately, it failed.

A brilliant account of what happened is chronicled in the book *The Rugby War* by Peter FitzSimons. FitzSimons was a powerful second-row forward, leading a nomadic existence in the mid-1980s, playing in Italy and France before returning to Australia in 1989 and representing his country in seven Tests. He became a full-time journalist with the *Sydney Morning Herald* in 1989 and has written many articles for the *Daily Telegraph*. FitzSimons develops the story in his book, examining 'how three determined men came within one hour of pulling off the sporting heist of the century ... and how another three men stopped them'.

Ross Turnbull was another larger-than-life Australian. He played for his country at rugby and became a prominent administrator with NSW and the ARU. He represented Australia on the IRB and would probably have become one of the most influential Australian Rugby Union administrators of all time but fell foul of the Union over major problems with the Concord Oval in Sydney and had to resign his various posts and became an outsider looking in.

Turnbull's version of events obviously differs from the Union hierarchy and as the WRC never, in the end, succeeded, no one will know whether Turnbull should be portrayed as an altruistic, misunderstood innovator or a chancer who saw millions of dollars to be made by exploiting the greed and/or frustration (depending on your point of view) of rugby players worldwide.

When we interviewed Turnbull, he said that the players had lost respect for the administrators in the 1990s and he masterminded the WRC to stop Rupert Murdoch's Super League signing up the world's best rugby players, thereby stopping the Super League scouts dead in their tracks. Turnbull claims that he saw what Murdoch had done with American Football in the early 1990s and, when Murdoch came back to Australia to promote Super League, Turnbull realised that, if nobody saw what was happening and tried to counter it, then the game would be lost.

The IRB takes its time to act (even FitzSimons said in his book that the IRB was 'missing in action' when the whole drama was unfolding) and the one common factor was that time was a precious commodity.

Kerry Packer's lawyer, Geoff Levy, asked Turnbull to put together a plan for professional rugby and he did it in five days. Packer approved the plan and, through senior players in the major countries, the WRC 'signed up' 501 of the world's best rugby players in apparently two weeks.

Turnbull maintains that 'Murdoch's idea was to take rugby league around the world and there was certainly a grand design. A lot of Wallabies were signed up for rugby league as were a number of New Zealanders. We arrived in South Africa to let them know quietly that there was another option to Super League. During the Rugby World Cup, the SANZAR countries announced the big deal with TV but I knew it was nowhere near enough money. It was not difficult for us to sign up the world's best players and stop Super League in its tracks

'I became Public Enemy Number 1, particularly in New Zealand, but WRC was the catalyst for change and everything that has happened since on the playing side and in administration was caused by the game having to rethink its future.'

Needless to say, there are other versions of events. In conversations with Phil Harry and Bruce Hayman, they asserted that the 'Turnbull Plan' was put together in April 1995 and that he was at a TV symposium in the USA trying to get backing for it from US money. The ARU obtained a copy of the plan and viewed it in detail. It was clear that it could not work as the location of 'constructed' teams with players drafted from all over the world to play in what were effectively non-playing rugby countries made the playing schedules impossible. Having costed the proposals, there was no way they were financially viable and the estimated crowd numbers were completely unrealistic.

Bruce Hayman made known to one of the Sydney sports journalists that such a document existed before the Australian squad left for South Africa. This was to ensure that the issue and Ross Turnbull's involvement in it became public knowledge. It was also the case that he was requiring everyone to sign a secrecy agreement before he would divulge any information to them.

According to Harry and Hayman, to suggest that he came up with a proposal that resulted in 501 players being signed up in two weeks was complete fabrication! Turnbull did not get the All Black signatures until well after the World Cup. This was well after Harry and Hayman had announced the SANZAR deal and had the money contract signed.

They also doubt that Turnbull could raise the funds needed to run a non-national-based competition. It should also be understood that Packer always maintained a complete disdain for the game of Union. He said in late 1994, when asked if he was interested in the Australian rights for his Channel 9 free-to-air network, 'Why would I want those rights? Rugby is a stupid game played by a bunch of fucking poofters ...' (Both James Erskine of IMG and Bruce Hayman can vouch for the veracity of this quote, word for word.) Harry and Hayman always maintained that Packer's only real interest in WRC was so that he could run interference against Murdoch after the SANZAR deal had been announced. Their view was that his desire was to trade off against Super League, so he could bring his Australian League rights back into value.

Another critic of the WRC was Simon Poidevin. Simon, a back-row forward, had played and captained Australia during the amateur days and became a successful businessman. He was also a part-time broadcaster and a great admirer of Sam Chisholm, Murdoch's supremo at News Corp.

Poidevin was one of the people who persuaded Chisholm and Ian Frykberg to invest in rugby union via a TV deal for the SANZAR countries. A deal was concluded on the eve of the World Cup in 1995, but with the advent of the WRC, Chisholm had the TV rights for the SANZAR countries but no players. Poidevin thought that Turnbull had hijacked the game and worked out that the WRC could not function without the South Africans. François Pienaar, who was representing most of the South African players, was due to attend a closed-circuit TV conference meeting between the players' leaders in the three Southern hemisphere countries. Pienaar was 'talked to' by News Corp executives, as well as Ian Frykberg and Poidevin. When Pienaar was not available for the three-way TV meeting, that spelled the start of the end of the WRC.

Someone who fought tooth and nail for rugby union in Australia was Bob Dwyer, who lost his job as coach of the national side to Greg Smith. It was not a big surprise that Dwyer's services were dispensed with, but that Smith was chosen by the board of the ARU ahead of John Connelly, the successful coach of Queensland, was a very big surprise.

Bob Dwyer is a man of many sides. He can be as prickly as a hedgehog and is not known as 'Barbed Wire' for nothing. He is a great conversationalist, a true student of the game and a very good host. His man-management style is entirely different to that of his late, lamented, regular second-in-command, Bob Templeton, but he is intensely loyal to his charges. He has a massive desire to win and has his own views on most subjects, expressing them without fear or favour, often finding that this polarises his supporters and detractors; some believe him to be very shrewd, while others see him as an over-opinionated motor-mouth.

He was the coach of Australia when they came to the UK in 1998. The tour started disastrously, with losses in England against the Northern Division, London and England, in Will Carling's first game as captain. But, with a dressing down of the squad which would have made Mike Tyson flinch, he got the show back on the road and the Wallabies went on undefeated for the rest of the tour. The following year, he took the side to France, and enjoyed a famous win against the French national side in Strasbourg.

1991 saw his greatest achievement with the winning of the World Cup, but the failure to beat England in the quarter-final of the 1995 tournament spelled the end of his reign, particularly as he had not endeared himself to the ARU officials with the support of the WRC circus.

Bob had spells of coaching in France at Stade Français, Leicester and Bristol in England, but is now back in Australia as Head Coach of the New South Wales State side.

Bob's views about the WRC option reinforced his controversial nature, and shows that not everyone who felt passionately about the game believed the WRC to be the devil incarnate. 'In spite of what others may say, the catalyst for the game going professional was Kerry Packer. We would have stuttered, stammered and procrastinated for years. I was in favour of what happened with the WRC because I thought this was the only way to get the IRB to the table. This was a battle between the two media moguls, Packer and Murdoch, and, in the end, they came to a handshake agreement – you have rugby union and I have horse racing – so rugby was a pawn in the game between two media giants.'

Dick McGruther saw the battle of Super League in rugby league as a very important influence on what happened in rugby union. Super League was a fight between News Corp and the establishment, one trying to protect their player base and the other trying to buy players. Part of the Super League plan was to recruit a number of high-profile Union players.

The ARU had a crisis meeting in Sydney in April 1995 when a statement was made that the game was no longer amateur, and that they did not have the players under control or contract. Packer in the 1970s had players contracted in cricket and he controlled the game. It took the ARU six months to ensure that all its players were under contract and the financial consequences were severe. Ninety per cent of the money they were getting from the News Corp TV deal was going to the players.

People like Bruce Hayman were incandescent about what Turnbull was trying to do with the WRC. At the dinner to mark 100 matches between Australia and New Zealand, he used the occasion to make a speech denouncing the actions of Turnbull to hijack rugby union. 'Whilst we hear plans to create a circus style of competition, we must ask: Who will be interested in following it? What we have seen here tonight, over 100 Test matches between Australia and New Zealand cannot be created. It must develop and evolve, for what makes established rugby competitions and matches such as Bledisloe Cup and European Five Nations so magical is the history and prestige that surrounds them. You can't replace 100 years of fierce rivalry and national pride with created teams which lack support and purpose and which are motivated only by the dollar.'

The players sat in silence. They would not look the ARU officials in the eye and, although it should have been an occasion for joyous celebration, it became a wake.

Australia was ahead in its thinking about professionalism. For instance, in 1993, Bob Dwyer, then coaching the national side, wrote a piece that was used in the magazine *Rugby World*, suggesting that the game would definitely go professional and no one should waste time arguing about it. As Dwyer has since said, 'For the most part, people took absolutely no notice whatsoever until professionalism was thrust upon us. In terms of Northern and Southern hemispheres, the North had about one month to get ready for professional rugby and the South about six years. But professionalism is more than about paying money. New Zealand became professional in their approach to the game around about 1986/7. Not in terms of payment to players, but in their attitude. Australia had to follow this attitude in preparation of teams and, by 1989, Australia had in place a fairly good professional structure.'

The Southern hemisphere definitely embraced professionalism quicker than the North, but the North was put on track due mainly to the clubs. For clubs in

England read Super 12 (the competition had been extended from ten to twelve provinces in 1996). The game has taken off at international level in Australia. The amount of spectator interest at the games and on television is staggering. In 1987, 18,000 turned up for an Australian Test match. In 2000, there were 110,000.

Rugby union is closing the gap between itself and League and Rules. Test matches, which were traditionally only played in Brisbane and Sydney, are now played in Melbourne and Perth. Spectators, television ratings and sponsorship are all up. Even Network Seven, a terrestrial broadcaster, has thrown its weight behind rugby, whereas previously AFL was its main winter sport.

Union has gained ground due mainly to the skills of John O'Neill, the General Manager of the ARU and also people like the ex-President Phil Harry. The ARU is run on professional lines, dispensing with bureaucratic committees and saw its revenue of A$9m in 1996 grow to a total of around A$60m in 2002. When the Lions played the deciding Third Test at Stadium Australia in Sydney in July 2001, more than 2 million watched Channel 7's live broadcast, which was more than watched the highest-rating State of Origin match. The three rugby union Tests averaged 1.6 million viewers and the three State of Origin rugby league games on the Nine network averaged 1.52 million.

Under a revamped four-year collective-bargaining agreement, Test, Super 12 and Australian Sevens players have been handed increased minimum salaries and a better average salary which makes them better paid than their cricket, AFL or rugby league counterparts

However, below the Super 12 level, the game has been left behind. Club rugby in the Southern hemisphere is compared to that of the second division level in England and France. It was always a social game, great exercise and afforded great camaraderie. Club sides in Sydney have fielded ten teams per week, that's 12 clubs in a city of 4 million people fielding seven or more senior sides with five Colts sides each weekend. This has now suffered and there is a lot of work to do to stop a further decline.

The most successful club side in New South Wales has been Randwick, which has had a vast roll-call of internationals over the years but has found it difficult in the professional era to get the internationals to come back and play for them when they are not playing State or international rugby.

As Bob Dwyer says, 'We have been at odds in Australia in how to handle this third level of rugby below country and State. We are questioning whether we should have a national competition with eight teams. The clubs do not want to lose further status. The clubs' presidents are almost invariably for the status quo. There is no money going down to that level, except a small amount to pay for a full-time Director of Rugby – that's all. We have got to make certain that the players stick by their contract that says they must play for their club once the international and State games have finished.

'Evolution can occur, but it is generally influenced by

outside forces and this is what has got to happen with the clubs. The players need a very clear understanding of what they are signing on to do.

'In cricket, there is the Australian team, the State team and the club competition. In Sydney, there are around 20 cricket first division clubs and a high number of grades. The role of that club is to provide a professional environment where a player can realise his potential and then a player knows that is his way forward.

'The same should apply in rugby, whereby if he joins a particular club, he will get the best possible preparation to help him in his rugby if he aspires to the professional game. In cricket, there are one or two professionals in each side. Under the 12 main Sydney rugby clubs, we have the umbrella of the sub-district clubs which are the smaller clubs that have been around since the year dot. Most only want to train once a week, but those who want to aspire to the professional game must have a clear route to the top and the junior clubs must not be competing with the first division clubs.

'My job is to make New South Wales as strong as it can be and coach the team, but after being a team coach I want to see a much more aggressive way of developing the club system with the ARU paying for a club coach and a fitness coach, as well as the Director of Rugby.'

The President of one of the oldest and best clubs in Australia, the Sydney University Rugby Club, reporting at the end of the 2000 season, was very wary of any change: 'There have been many changes at the NSWRU. We will provide whatever help we can in both the interests of NSW and our own club's rugby. We believe a strong NSWRU is critical for Australian rugby and the Sydney Competition. It will provide opportunities to our élite athletes which we strongly support.'

David Moffett has had a very interesting administrative career in sport. He was born in England but emigrated to Australia in his teens. He was a rugby referee and worked for the NSWRU. While there, he was one of the prime architects in the development of SANZAR, which saw the three Southern hemisphere countries putting together the 'Perfect Rugby Product' to sell to television.

Moffett moved on to New Zealand and became CEO of the Union which went through massive changes from a Council of 19 with 23 committees to a Board of nine. This was the result of a report by the Boston Consulting Group and Moffett was charged with putting it all together. There was no transitional plan and the game in New Zealand cost some of their good people their positions. However, during Moffett's five years in New Zealand, he took the Union from a A$6m loss in 1995 to a A$70m surplus at the end of 1999. He was also involved with others in a five-year US$100m deal with Adidas to sponsor the All Blacks.

Moffett then moved back to Australia and became CEO of National Rugby League. He had the task of resuscitating the National League after the mid-1990s 'Super League war'. He streamlined the League into a 14-team competition and signed a A$400m Pay TV contract, although he did not stay long enough to see the implementation of a strategic plan developed to take the game forward.

An insight into Moffett's thinking offers a clear idea of why he thinks that what he is doing in Wales is correct. 'If I was in charge in England, I would start with a clean sheet of paper and restructure. The owners are businessmen and they know what they are getting into, so they have got to expect changes. What you have got to do is check your egos in at the door and devise something that can cover the players, competitions, internationals, etc. Take out all the overseas players, reduce the number of teams so that they all compete in the European competition. All Wallabies and All Blacks play in the Super 12s, but a number of England internationals do not play in Europe because their side does not qualify.'

Club owners in Wales, does this sound familiar?

There is no doubt the antipodean thinking was on a different planet from the Northern hemisphere about the state of the game and the way forward. That's why the Southern hemisphere hatched their grand plan for the survival of rugby union in the jungle of professional sport.

Sam Chisholm was Murdoch's supremo in television outside America. So in the company of the man they were relying on to bring home the bacon, Ian Frykberg of CSI, one of the best negotiators in the sports business, the officials from the three main Southern hemisphere countries met Chisholm on 16 May 1995. A few weeks later, on the eve of the World Cup Final between South

Africa and New Zealand, at a press conference in the trophy room at the Ellis Park Stadium, Johannesburg, an announcement was made that News Corp had bought the television rights for ten years to all internationals and provincial rugby in the three countries for US$555m. Money was talking ... BIG money. A media mogul had flexed his muscles and he was about to change the face of the last of the major worldwide team games.

In retrospect, did SANZAR sell too quickly and for too little? The £370 million, ten-year deal worked out at £11 million per annum for the three countries. Compare this with England's five-year deal with Sky of £87.5 million which gave it £17.5 million per annum. In the end the SANZAR officials had to make decisions almost on the run and even if the deal was too long and too cheap it gave them the critical breathing space to thwart both Turnbull and the development of rugby league. And it gave them, for the first time, a greater power within the IRB. It also made the decision-making progress in Paris in August 1995 inevitable.

7

RAISING THE WORLD CUP

We cannot be absolutely certain as to who had the idea for a Rugby World Cup first.

In Australia, the feeling is, according to rugby legend Sir Nick Shehadie, that Harold Tolhurst a former international wing and referee, was banging on about a world tournament as far back as 1957. Twenty-odd years later, the former President of the ARU, Bill McLaughlin, noted in 1979 that the Australian Bicentennial celebrations were due in 1988. He thought it would be a good idea for the ARU to organise a World Cup by invitation at the same time.

The Kiwis, not to be outdone, had also been considering some kind of world tournament. Ivan Vodanovich, the former All Black and a member of the

1987 NZRFU World Cup Committee, told Derek Wyatt back in 1994 that he thought that Pat Gill, a New Zealand Council member and Chairman of the Players' Committee, had been the mover and shaker behind it. Certainly, Ces Blazey, the President of the NZRFU, had it in mind because, like McLaughlin, he had submitted a request to hold a World Cup to the IRB.

The IRB was a gentlemen's club, and not much interested in the democratic process. It was decidedly unworldly. It favoured the four Home Unions and allowed the old colonies in, but did not intially give them the same weight of votes. Yet as the record shows, time and again, the Home Unions lost out to their Southern neighbours home and away. And the Lions fared no better until 1971. In some ways, then, it should have come as no surprise that the so-called upstart countries of Australia and New Zealand should be thinking about a World Cup. They were closer to the game. The surprise, if there was one, was that they both applied for it without telling one another. Both, clearly, were aware of their place in history.

But, at the beginning of the 1980s, there were other forces in town. An Australian entrepreneur by the name of David Lord had signed up, it was alleged, 212 out of 217 of the world's leading Union players. Kerry Packer, the Australian media magnate, had a few years earlier split cricket in two. Around 1977–78, he had contracted cricket professionals from England, Australia, West Indies, India, Pakistan and New Zealand. Separate Test matches were played alongside those of the official cricket authorities. Packer threatened cricket's hegemony. He was a catalyst who shook cricket's conservatism to the core.

Lord had much the same thing in mind. He wanted a professional circus based on the Packer model and he wanted to start it preferably for the 1982–83 season Down Under. Time was pressing and, as rugby union was always under pressure from rugby league, the last thing it could afford was a schism within its own ranks. But Lord did not have the resources of Packer.

Meanwhile, in London, the bug had also bitten Neil Durden-Smith, a sports entrepreneur, and throughout 1982–83 he canvassed heavily for a World Cup to be held in the four Home Unions. There must have been something in the water.

Sir Nick Shehadie had now become President of the ARU. During a weekend away at a favourite resort, six senior Wallabies showed Shehadie their contracts with Lord. Shehadie had only one option left: to persuade the IRB to hasten the decision on a World Cup. He also couldn't really afford to upset the All Blacks and, on the basis that half a cake's better than no cake at all, he met Ces Blazey and Russ Thomas of the NZRFU in Auckland and, while updating them on the Lord scenario, he also proposed a joint bid to the IRB for a World Cup.

The IRB was never particularly quick on the uptake; it was always off the pace. It was still struggling with the concept of a permanent home and secretariat. Yet it was going to have to respond to the demands from Down Under. While the IRB dithered, another world body, the

IAAF, had organised its first Track and Field World Cup in Helsinki in 1983.

Two offers were on the table for a World Cup for 1988. The ARU had put its bid in to an emergency meeting of the IRB on 25 June 1983, and New Zealand had followed in March 1984. Meanwhile, David Lord's threat had subsided. He had come close to creating a breakaway, but in the end uncertainty crept in amongst a number of the players and the audacious heist failed.

Eventually, the IRB, as ever, gave away a spectacular penalty try, when it asked the representatives from Australia and New Zealand to come forward with a proposal for the Board's next meeting in March 1985. The die had been cast. The matter was on the agenda. Dr Roger Vanderfield, then the Aussie Chairman of the IRB, disclosed, 'It was a mistake by the four Home Unions to ask for a report. The report was only their stay of execution. What I didn't know was how the 16 members would vote come 1985, and so we undertook some discreet lobbying.' This did not stop Albert Ferrasse, the French President of the FFR, from making a late bid for a World Cup in France!

At the IRB meeting in March 1985, Australia, New Zealand, South Africa and France all voted for the World Cup – 8–0; Ireland and Scotland voted against – 8–4. The representatives for England and Wales split their votes, and so a World Cup was born with the final voting: 10 for and 6 against.

Undoubtedly, the members for England and Wales voted against the wishes of their respective Unions; the voting ought to have been tied at eight-all. But it was too late; the first Rugby World Cup was born and was to be held not, unfortunately, in 1988 (because of the Seoul Olympics) nor in 1989, as the Lions were due to tour Australia, nor 1990 (because of the FIFA World Cup in Italy), but amazingly in 1987, just two years away.

There was a mass of work that needed to be agreed once the decision of the IRB became public. The IRB members were virgins when it came to appreciating the value of television rights and sponsorship. Interestingly, neither ISL, the Lucerne-based sports agency, nor Neil Durden-Smith's company, made it to the short list to represent the tournament. Three did – West Nally (a London-based company headed by Patrick Nally), IMG (Mark McCormack's lot) and a consortia put together by Ross Turnbull on behalf of the NSWRFU.

The IRB asked for a deposit of US$5 million. IMG hesitated. The consortia from NSWRFU was backed by Murdoch (now there's a surprise) but only Turnbull was in the loop. As he was still an IRB Board member and Australia was a host country, his proposals were not taken seriously (but no doubt the experience gave Turnbull some food for thought for the future; at least he was capable of thinking outside the box). Only West Nally provided the down-payment. Or at least a company called Strathmore Holdings, then listed on the Auckland stock exchange, did. Strathmore lent Patrick Nally the money for the deposit.

The IRB made many mistakes in the lead up to the first World Cup. But they made one crucial decision, which was to save their bacon. The down-payment of US$5 million had to be paid in instalments and had to be completed before the World Cup was under way. So, when Strathmore (and later West Nally) went under, the 1987 organising committee was rejoicing at its good fortune and cleverness in its contractual obligations. It was about their only success.

Meanwhile, Ross Turnbull made one further attempt at a coup at an IRB meeting in Los Angeles on 18 July 1986, and so very nearly succeeded when he proposed a new and dynamic committee to run the World Cup, but the voting was four-all and the Chairman, John Kendall-Carpenter, the headmaster from Wellington School in Somerset, cast his vote for the status quo.

When you think that the reason why New Zealand dropped out of hosting the Rugby World Cup in 2003 was because of the problems of making sure its stadiums were 'clean', it should not come as too much of a surprise that this was also an issue in 1987!

Another fight, which has again resurfaced in 2003, was the right of the host countries to keep the gate receipts. This set a precedent for the World Cup in 1991, but, by 1995 in South Africa, the IRB had clawed back 50 per cent of the receipts. As a result of the clean stadium issue, Australia could not host the final at the Sydney Cricket Ground, which gave New Zealand a fortuitous boost, for she could provide clean stadiums and therefore hosted the final at Eden Park in Auckland. In 1987, 1991 and 1995, the host nation reached the final; in two of these finals they were to win it, too!

For the Rugby World Cup in 1987, hosted jointly by Australia and New Zealand, the essential problem then for the ARU and the NZRFU was that neither of them owned their major stadiums, unlike Wales, Ireland, England and Scotland. Their provincial Unions owned their grounds. If this wasn't ultimately to be such a headache, the real mistake of the 1987 World Cup was to allow two countries to host the tournaments. As it was, the distribution of the Pools was bizarre in the extreme. Pool A was based in Sydney and Brisbane; Pool B in Napier, Wellington, Palmerston North, Dunedin, Invercargill and Brisbane; Pool C in Auckland, Hamilton, Wellington, Christchurch and Dunedin; and Pool D in Auckland, Christchurch, Wellington and Dunedin.

Fourteen invited teams joined Australia and New Zealand in the third week of May 1987 to kick-start the first Rugby World Cup. There were ten countries from the Northern hemisphere and six from the Southern. Teams were placed in four Pools; in Pool A were Australia, England, USA and Japan; in Pool B, Wales, Ireland, Canada and Tonga; in Pool C, New Zealand, Fiji, Italy and Argentina; and in Pool D, France, Scotland, Romania and Zimbabwe. The draw was unfavourable to the old guard of the four Home Unions; they could have reasonably expected to be placed in each of the four pools but, instead, Wales and Ireland were thrown together in Pool B. From each pool, two teams would go through to the knock-out stages.

Coming into the tournament, the world rankings were:

1. NZ
2. Australia
3. France
4. Scotland
5. England
6. Wales
7. Ireland
8. Romania
9. Argentina
10. Fiji
11. Tonga
12. Italy
13. Canada
14. Japan
15. USA
16. Zimbabwe

South Africa was still a pariah country and unable to play in either Australia or New Zealand for justifiable political reasons. Had she been allowed, she would have been ranked sixth. The USSR was originally invited but pulled out, hence Zimbabwe's strange inclusion. The USSR could, on occasions give Romania a hard game and would have been ranked thirteenth.

It is hard to believe that less than 20 years ago there were so few countries of stature playing rugby union. In truth, the game had become the domain of the four Home Unions who were throttling its development. They were of the view that what mattered was not rugby world cups (all six of the votes against such an event were cast by them) but the British (and Irish) Lions tours.

On the basis of the rankings, it would not have been difficult to predict that Australia and England, Wales and Ireland, New Zealand and Argentina and France (Grand Slam winners at home) and Scotland would go through to the quarter-finals and, but for a small hiccup in Pool C, that was how it panned out. There was one game of merit – France's draw with Scotland 20–20 (when tries were worth four points); otherwise, the All Blacks notwithstanding, the games were poor. In their pool, Fiji, Italy and Argentina all managed a win each and so Fiji went through on point difference. And, because they had scored more tries in their game with Scotland, France was judged the winner of Pool D.

The quarter-finals were thus: Australia v Ireland, Wales v England, New Zealand v Scotland and France v Fiji.

In each case, the Pool winners went through to the semi-finals. Australia beat Ireland without breaking sweat, 33-15; Wales easily outsmarted a desperate England 16-3; New Zealand had still to be challenged and won leisurely against Scotland 30-3 and, finally, France overcame a strong Fijian side in a difficult match, winning 31-16.

So, fortunately for the television audience, the semi-finals involved two countries from the Northern hemisphere and two from the Southern. Australia was at home to France in Sydney and the All Blacks were due to entertain Wales in Brisbane. The final was set to be

Australia versus New Zealand just as the administrators had planned it back in 1979. The bulk of the Wallaby side (except the Ella brothers) was made up from their brilliant Grand Slam team of 1984, yet Australia had won only six of the 14 fixtures against New Zealand in the 1980s. The world waited for them both to win through to what would be an absorbing final.

As we all know, what attracts pundits to watching live sport is the fact that anything can happen. And so it proved. Australia blew up against France and succumbed at home 30-24, thanks to the wayward brilliance of a last-minute try by Serge Blanco in what was an amazing match. New Zealand strolled through their semi-final against Wales, winning 49-6; they had still to be tested. Maurice Trapp, an Auckland coach, said, 'If the four Home Unions only want social rugby, then they shouldn't bother coming to the World Cup.' He had a point.

The final was not a showpiece. They rarely are. New Zealand, in the end, easily beat France 29-9. It was a contest only in the first half. France's semi-final had taken its toll. But it was important for New Zealand that they won. The country needed healing after the 1981 flour bomb Test against the Springboks; after the 1985 court case where Paddy Finnegan and Phillip Recordon stopped the All Blacks from touring South Africa; and the subsequent 1986 tour when Andy Haden's Cavaliers cavaliered against the spirit of the game in apartheid South Africa.

RWC1987 played to huge crowds in New Zealand and,

by winning it, confirmed to every Kiwi what they have always known – that the game belongs to them.

There were many lessons to be learned from the inaugural tournament. The IRB needed to become professionalised and it required its own full-time secretariat and a permanent home. The opening ceremony was appalling and this had to be remedied. There seemed little point in the play-off game for third place unless it was accompanied by a win bonus and automatic qualification for the subsequent World Cup and, most of all, it was widely agreed that any future World Cups were never again to be hosted by more than one country.

*   *   *

The 1991 Rugby World Cup was held in five countries, with four legal systems, three different currencies, two different languages and one ball. You couldn't make it up. It was clear that the IRB was bent on self-destruction. Once again, there were four pools of four and the countries qualifying were exactly the same as in 1987, except Western Samoa appeared instead of Tonga. The old IRB countries had been given automatic qualification by way of reaching the quarter-final stages in RWC1987; the other eight had to pre-qualify in tournaments in the Americas (USA, Argentina and Canada), Africa (Zimbabwe), Asia (Japan), Europe (Italy and Romania) and Australasia (Western Samoa). These tournaments were a breath of fresh air and were hugely welcomed by the lesser-developed rugby-playing countries, as it gave them an opportunity not just to play but also to lobby their governments for extra resources.

The world rankings for RWC1991 were:

1. Australia
2. New Zealand
3. England
4. France
5. Ireland
6. Scotland
7. Wales
8. Canada
9. Argentina
10. Italy
11. Western Samoa
12. Fiji
13. Romania
14. USA
15. Japan
16. Zimbabwe.

In Pool A, England, New Zealand, Italy and USA played matches at Twickenham, Otley, Gloucester and Leicester.

In Pool B, Scotland, Japan, Zimbabwe and Ireland played matches at Murrayfield, Lansdowne Road and Belfast.

In Pool C, Wales, Australia, Argentina and Western Samoa played matches at the Arms Park, Llanelli, Pontypool and Pontypridd.

In Pool D, France, Fiji, Canada and Romania played matches in the South of France at Beziers, Bayonne, Grenoble, Toulouse, Brive and Agen.

The tournament began with a pathetic ceremony at Twickenham just before the opening game between England (hosting the eventual final) and New Zealand (the holders). In a dour game, the All Blacks edged it 18-12. Once again, it looked as if the old nations would reach the quarter-final stages – Pool A was a no-brainer for the All Blacks and England; Pool B, ditto for Scotland and Ireland; in Pool C, Wales might have a tough game against Argentina but they ought to go through with Australia; and in Pool D, France should qualify with Fiji or emerging Canada.

Once again, the pundits misread their tea leaves. There were surprises in both Pools C and D. Amazingly, Western Samoa beat Wales 16-13 at the Arms Park. As some wag put it, 'Goodness knows what the score would have been if Wales had played the whole of Samoa.' Worse was to come when the Wallabies subsequently thrashed them 35-12, making up for the loss they suffered for third place in RWC1987. This was the beginning of the end of Wales being a top-flight rugby nation.

In Pool D, Canada edged out both Fiji and Romania and only just lost to France 19-13. Rather like New Zealand in RWC1987, the French took the game to the regions and were rewarded with packed crowds and huge media interest. In the four Home Unions, the Western Samoan result against Wales set the tongues wagging and ITV, the host broadcaster, at last had a story to tell.

A growing worry was the discrepancies in the scores between matches involving the IRB countries and the lesser countries. In RWC1987, England had beaten Japan 60-7; New Zealand had exhausted Italy 70-6, and Fiji 74-13; France had beaten Zimbabwe 70-12. In RWC1991, Ireland beat Zimbabwe 55-11 and even Japan beat Zimbabwe 52-8. There was a need to embrace the lesser countries, perhaps in a tournament of their own. This has still to happen and, just to make the point in RWC1995, for instance, there were runaway wins for New Zealand against Japan 145-17, and by Scotland and France against the Ivory Coast 89-0 and 54-18 respectively. It repeated itself in RWC1999, when New Zealand beat Italy 101-3 and England beat Tonga 103-10.

The quarter finals in RWC1991 pitted Pools A v D and B v C, which was a small change to RWC1987. So New Zealand played Canada at Lille, France; Scotland played Western Samoa at Murrayfield, Scotland; Australia played Ireland at Lansdowne Road, Dublin; and France played England at Parc des Princes, Paris.

A betting man would have concluded that the All Blacks would take out Canada, that Western Samoa might shock the Jocks but that their wisdom should see them through, that Ireland could cause the biggest upset, even though the Wallabies were hot to trot, and that either side could win in Paris, but the home side ought to start as favourites.

RWC1991 came of age with these quarter-final matches. They were titanic struggles. With six minutes to go in Dublin, Ireland led Australia 18-14 but were still beaten; in a bruising, ill-tempered encounter in Paris where the English forwards recalled Agincourt and more, they took the game 19-10; Canada pushed the All Blacks but lost 29-13; only Scotland went with the script, beating a mentally tired Western Samoa 28-6. So, we were left with two mouth-watering semi-finals – Australia v New Zealand in Dublin and Scotland v England at Murrayfield. How lucky we were. Once again, the media marvelled at a prospective final that would pitch a Northern hemisphere country against its Southern counterpart.

On Saturday, 26 October 1991, the 'auld enemy' took on England at Murrayfield. It was a tense, nerve-racking game, with both sides freezing at critical times. In the end, it came down to a drop goal, which clinched the game for England as they went through 9-6, both teams having kicked two penalties apiece. Just as Wales's loss to Western Samoa was a marker, so was Scotland's against England; she would never again be in the top flight of rugby countries. Attention now turned to Dublin on the next day for the second of the semi-finals.

Sports psychologists will confirm that, in team sports, there has to be success on and off the field. The management must be as one. In the All Black camp, there were widely reported schisms between the coaches and the players. The Australian team stayed put in Dublin for its epic encounter with New Zealand and toured hospitals and schools, building a relationship with the Irish who then turned up in their droves to cheer them on against their keenest rivals. David Campese had one of those games from his ever-expanding top draw that he'd remember long after retirement. Many thought that this was the final that they would have liked to see, but once the All Blacks had accounted for England in their first game, it was never going to be. For this to happen, New Zealand should have been in Pool B.

The Wallabies played the All Blacks in the semi-final. They had lost 6-3 against them two months earlier in Auckland and the game marked the 40th Test partnership between Farr-Jones and Lynagh. In a marvellous game, the Wallabies won 16-6, inflicting the third Test defeat on the All Blacks since 1987. The Australians were in the final. This set up a game against England about which David Campese was quoted as saying, 'England would never beat us in the World Cup because they are a bunch of toffs and we are convicts.'

The RWC1991 final at Twickenham saw England play the more fancied Australians. Before the team went out on to the field to face England, the genial Bob Templeton, Assistant Coach to Bob Dwyer, read a poem, written by Peter Fenton, called 'The Running Game'.

There is a spirit in the Wallabies
Mere words cannot describe,
It's as if they had descended
From some legendary tribe.

There's a kinship, a tradition
As in days so long since past,

Of crusaders, of knights in armour
And of men before the mast.
There's a thrill you cannot appreciate,
A pride you cannot tell,
Lest you wear your nation's jumper
And you wear it really well.

When you mark before the forward rush,
So doing, turn the tide,
When you make that vital tackle
And your line is open wide.
When you go down on the rolling ball
And dare the trampling feet,
When you lift your aching body
And the opposition meet.

When you burst away from tacklers
And you make the winning run,
And you come back heart a'thumping
And your team-mates say, 'Well done.'

But it isn't just the winning
Nor the score, nor the cheers,
It's the friendship and the memories
That last you through the years.

It's the camaraderie
That's born of valour, not of fame,
It's the sheer exhilaration
When you play the running game.

History will tell us that the Wallabies triumphed 12-6 in a game which only reached the heights on a few occasions. But it certainly propelled Australian rugby to heights it had not known before. The French rugby newspaper, *Midi Olympique*, named six Australians in its world rugby top ten and Don Cameron, writing in the *New Zealand Herald*, wrote that the Wallabies were the best organised, most talented and enterprising international side in rugby at the time. Farr-Jones became a hero, 'Captain Courageous' as he was dubbed. The team had a tickertape parade in Sydney, Farr-Jones was presented with the key of the city by the Lord Mayor of Sydney and many other honours were bestowed on the Wallabies.

Australia loves a winner and, as a country, has had many in all kinds of sports. But now the rugby union side, those 'rah rah' guys who still had jobs to hold down in addition to their sporting endeavours, were winners. They had disappointed in the inaugural World Cup in 1987 but were now kings of the castle and many Australians, who had never seen a rugby union game in their lives, wanted to feel part of the success. Australian rugby union was on a roll.

The final was a rich experience for those of us able to enjoy it. But, behind the scenes, the IRB showed its true colours. They were lucky to have got out of jail for a second time as they almost gave the tournament away.

*   *   *

The Rainbow Nation, as President Mandela was fond of describing South Africa, hosted RWC1995. This was a first for the post-apartheid country. It was a first in other ways, too – the first World Cup to be in one country, which meant one set of lawyers and one currency. No wonder it was easily the best World Cup to date. Still, South Africa was not the outright favourite at the start of the competition, that was the preserve of the magical All Blacks who were desperate to win again having won last in 1987.

The world rankings were:

1. New Zealand
2. Australia
3. France
4. South Africa
5. England
6. Scotland
7. Ireland
8. Wales
9. Western Samoa
10. Canada
11. Argentina
12. Italy
13. Tonga
14. Romania
15. Japan
16. Ivory Coast

There were four pools of four. Pool A, comprising South Africa, Australia, Canada and Romania played at Newlands (Cape Town), Port Elizabeth and Stellenbosch.

In Pool B, England, Western Samoa, Italy and Argentina played at East London and Durban.

In Pool C, New Zealand, Ireland, Wales and Japan played at Bloemfontein and Ellis Park (Johannesburg), 6,000ft above sea level

In Pool D, France, Scotland, Tonga and the Ivory Coast played at Rustenburg and Loftus Versfeld (Pretoria), also 6,000ft above sea level.

The opening ceremony and the opening game between South Africa (the hosts) and Australia (the Cup holders) gave spectators and television viewers alike a classic spectacle, perhaps the best ever of its kind, which sent the whole of the country into some kind of collective frenzy. President Mandela stayed and stayed (he was due to leave the game at half-time) to watch his side beat the Wallabies 27-18. What a start! The reigning champions had been truly dumped on.

The eventual pool winners were South Africa, England, New Zealand and France, with the runners-up being respectively Australia, Western Samoa, Ireland and Scotland. The only difference in RWC1995 to RWC1991 was that South Africa had made it through for the first time (it was their first appearance in a final) in place of Canada (but not before an unsavoury game between them). Once again, Wales failed to make it through to the last eight. The Wales–Ireland match was one of the most sterile witnessed in any World Cup to date. The form teams were South Africa, France and New Zealand.

Elsewhere, the All Blacks were their usual rampant

selves, beating Japan 145-17 and accounting for both Ireland (43-19) and Wales (34-9). There were some other large scores – Scotland thumped newcomers Ivory Coast 89-0, which was a tough way for the débutants to experience their first taste of world rugby. Worse was to follow when Max Brito was paralysed for life as a result of an injury sustained whilst playing for the Ivory Coast against Tonga. Scotland's narrow loss to France by 19-22 meant that, instead of playing Ireland in the next round, they were drawn against the All Blacks.

The quarter-final draw included France v Ireland, which France won comfortably 36-12. Indeed, such was France's form that many thought they would make it through to the finals. South Africa were too strong for Western Samoa (42-14), New Zealand duly disposed of Scotland 48-30, and Australia, surprisingly, came a cropper against a defiant England, thanks to a very late drop-goal by Rob Andrew (22-25). Australia had not fully recovered from their opening-day experience.

The consequence of these games pitched South Africa against France and New Zealand against England: or Southern hemisphere v Northern hemisphere.

The game between South Africa and France should never have taken place. The pitch was severely waterlogged and, although it went ahead, it was more water polo than rugby union. France should have refused to play. Had the game been delayed a day, the pitch would have made a recovery and a proper game would have ensued. The decision to play ultimately favoured South Africa as they swam for victory, winning 19-15, even though France had a try disallowed and played the better rugby. South Africa was waking up to the fact that they were just one game away from being World Champions, something they had always felt they had been in their apartheid days.

A day later and England were blown away by a giant of a man but a kid at heart, Jonah Lomu, the exciting new left-wing threequarter. He was everywhere and at half-time the score was 25-3. England weren't as fit, had no game plan for Lomu (he scored four tries) and looked a spent force. They rallied towards the end of the game so the final score line did not look so embarrassing at 42-29, but this was a game too far for England. They had flattered to deceive. They needed a major rethink.

And so the final was played at Ellis Park, some 6,000ft above sea level. The night before, a number of All Blacks suffered severe food poisoning and it showed in more ways than you'd care to think about on the field. But Mandela had his way as only he can and the 'Boks beat the favourites 12-9 after extra time. It was a tense final but, as with the opening win against Australia, the whole country partied. South Africa had won their first World Cup at the first attempt. They had hosted it in a way that brought the nation's diverse peoples together. And it had been hosted in the spirit of the game, too. At last, this was a World Cup that lived up to its promise and one that few who witnessed it will forget.

*   *   *

RWC1999 was hosted by Wales, but you wouldn't have known it. Once again, matches were spread across the Five Nations. Once again, this was a terrible mistake. As ever, there was some heavy politicking before Wales won the right to host the tournament.

After the 1995 World Cup in South Africa, there was a feeling, particularly among the Northern hemisphere hierarchy, that the 1999 World Cup should be north of the equator. Australia had never subscribed to the view that the extravaganza should alternate between hemispheres. They rather felt that the best bid should secure the tournament, whatever the location.

Bruce Hayman, one of the Australian officials charged with putting in a bid for the 1999 World Cup on behalf of Australia, reveals, 'We had a proposal for the 1999 World Cup which we felt was imaginative and exciting. Our proposal was based on Australia, but with one Pool in New Zealand and one Pool in Japan. We felt that, for the first time, a World Cup tournament of any code of rugby could be held in part of Asia.

'The opportunity for the Union game was enormous. Everyone was fighting tooth and nail in rugby league with the Super League and I believed if we had been able to say that we were going to have the RWC here in 1999, then rugby league would not exist today. We also thought that we would beat soccer in holding a major world tournament in Asia a few years ahead of them.'

Phil Harry, President of the ARU, felt that Australia was comfortably ahead in terms of votes. But a secret manoeuvre, a new bid from Wales involving five Pools instead of four, was put under the doors of the delegates the night before the votes were taken, although the Australian, New Zealand and Japanese delegates, strangely, did not find their copies until the next morning!

On the voting front, Australia had two votes, New Zealand two, Japan and Italy one vote each. France, who had two votes, had said they would vote for the Australian proposal. However, Bernard Lapasset, the French Rugby Federation President, told the Australian delegation that France was changing its votes. Up to that stage, Australia felt they would have had enough votes as Argentina had indicated that they would vote for them and, similarly, South Africa. Phil Harry says, 'We had good relations with South Africa and they always made the point that Australia had stood by them during the difficult years. However, at a late stage in the build-up to the vote, Louis Luyt, the SARFU President, made the point they would not vote for Australia because of the involvement of Japan.'

The initial Welsh bid showed four Pools. The fifth Pool emerged the night before the meeting, causing France to vote for Wales. South Africa then also indicated they would vote for Wales.

Bruce Hayman continues, 'We got our bid in on time and met every requirement. Not one word changed. The only thing that was not in our presentation, which was not material to the document, was that we wanted to hold a Plate competition for the losing eight teams as curtain-raisers to the main games. We saw this as a development aspect and the funds would come from ARU, and not RWC.'

Right up to the eve of the presentation, Australia was very confident of success but Phil Harry realised that the actions of Wales the night before had scuttled their bid. 'By the time we got up to do our presentation we realised that it would be a waste of time after the overnight change of proposal from Wales.

'In fact, the presentation went really well and was well received but it was obvious to us that the case had been lost. At the end of the presentation, I asked if I could make some closing remarks, which I did, and finished by saying, "The Australian Rugby Union reserves our rights." Keith Rowlands was involved in a whispered conversation and we were asked what we meant by "reserving our rights". We just repeated what we said and Vernon Pugh got very defensive. However, we were not prepared to say anything else as we were so mad that the whole process had been underhanded and, in our opinion, smacked of conspiracy.'

RWC1999 marked a different and more confusing enlargement of the tournament. The number of teams was extended from 16 to 20, bringing with it accusations of unfairness, which were totally justified. To reach the final, some teams would have to play three games in the opening round, a pre-qualifier for the quarter-finals, then a quarter-final followed by a semi and a final. Surprise, surprise, none of those countries that had to pre-qualify for the quarter-finals made it past the quarter-finals. Theirs was a game too far. RWC1999 almost marked the first professional World Cup since the game was declared open in August 1995.

The world rankings were:

1. New Zealand
2. Australia
3. South Africa
4. France
5. England
6. Ireland
7. Scotland
8. Wales
9. Argentina
10. Samoa
11. Fiji
12. Canada
13. Italy
14. Tonga
15. Romania
16. USA
17. Japan
18. Uruguay
19. Spain
20. Namibia

Pool A comprised South Africa, Scotland, Spain and Uruguay, and was played at Murrayfield, Galashiels and Glasgow.

Pool B involved New Zealand, England, Italy and

Tonga, with games at Twickenham, Huddersfield, Leicester and Bristol.

Pool C saw France, Canada, Fiji and Namibia play at Toulouse, Beziers and Bordeaux.

Pool D had Wales, Argentina, Samoa and Japan playing at Wrexham, Llanelli and Cardiff.

Pool E saw Australia, Ireland, the USA and Romania playing at Dublin, Belfast and Limerick.

Spain, Uruguay, Namibia and a united Samoa were making their World Cup débuts.

There were a number of games in the opening rounds where the major countries overwhelmed the junior nations. Fiji v Namibia ended 67-18; Australia v Romania, 57-9; Wales v Japan, 64-15; New Zealand v Italy, 101-3; Canada v Namibia, 73-11; and England v Tonga, 101-10. There must come a time when there are two World Cup tournaments, one for the professionals and one for the amateurs.

The Pool winners were South Africa (A), New Zealand (B), France (C), Wales (D) and Australia (E). This meant then that the runners-up from the five Pools – England, Fiji, Scotland, Ireland and Argentina – plus the best results from one country placed third (Samoa), went through to the rather ugly system of a pre-qualifier for the real thing, the quarter-finals. Thus, England beat Fiji 45-24 at Twickenham; Scotland beat Samoa 35-20 at Murrayfield and, the surprise so far of the tournament, Argentina beat Ireland 28-24 at Lens in France.

While the winners of the Pools had a week to prepare for their quarter-finals, those involved in the pre-qualifiers had to play a tough mid-week fixture. This was a mistake. There should have been four Pools of five countries with the top two qualifying as in previous World Cups.

RWC1999 was heralded by the IRB after the event as the biggest and best tournament, but it was a miserable failure. Unlike RWC1991, the tournament did not bring a new audience to the game or new spectators. And there was yet another ticketing fiasco. Scotland played in front of pitifully small crowds; it was as if they had learned nothing from the experiences of New Zealand (RWC1987) or France (RWC1991) in taking the games around their own country. It was a golden opportunity for the Scots, but they were hampered by the insistence of the IRB to maximise revenues. England played at Huddersfield (rugby league territory) but could not reduce the price of tickets so that schoolchildren and teachers could watch free. As a result, these games failed to sell out.

Whilst rugby union has slavishly followed its bigger brother soccer (as the 1998 FIFA World Cup in France demonstrated) in creating more and more preliminary rounds, there is a danger of spectators at home, for that is all that matters these days, developing viewing fatigue. World Cups only come to life at the sudden-death stages. RWC1999 was a very slow burn because the RWC Tournament Committee refused to have a media centre in London.

There may be some truth in the proposition that, when it comes to rugby, the Celts hate the English, but when

London is the only global city in the four Home Unions, it was selfish and remiss of all of them not to make use of it for their own long-term benefits, especially in building added value for would-be tourists. Derek Wyatt saw at first-hand the British Tourist Association's Welsh packages being offered through its Sydney offices on a visit in January 1999. Then, 85 per cent of visitors entering the four Home Unions did so through the three London termini of Heathrow, Gatwick and Stansted. During this same trip, he also visited the Melbourne Airport Duty Free Shop where the Sydney Olympic organising committee had already set up a purpose-built outlet; RWC1999 missed this trick and yet RWC1995 had shops in every major airport festooned with memorabilia (in fact, they were so successful they regularly ran out of popular items).

The 1999 Rugby World Cup came to life in the quarter-finals when South Africa beat a desperate England team 41-21 with Jannie de Beer setting a new record with no less than five drop goals. Earlier, Australia had accounted for Wales by 24-9 and what with France beating Argentina 47-20 and New Zealand making hard work of defeating Scotland 30-18, the semi-final matches lined up as South Africa v Australia and New Zealand v France, with the expectation that Australia and New Zealand would make the finals.

New Zealand had set off like a rocket (as they did in RWC1995) with wins against Tonga, England and Italy, but as they neared their goal of winning the cup they felt they had deserved in South Africa, the team seemed to be developing a collective bout of the jitters.

South Africa lost to Australia in the first semi-final on 30 October 1999. It was a game that could have gone either way, but the Wallabies' defence was outstanding. Larkham, Horan and Burke had important games, and Australia were in their second World Cup Final.

The next day at Twickenham, the All Blacks went into the changing rooms at half-time with a lead of 17-11, and just after half-time they added another converted try to put them 14 points ahead. All they had to do was carry on in much the same fashion and a place in the finals was theirs for the taking. And what was the final score? It may be difficult to believe but France trounced the All Blacks in one of the greatest comebacks ever seen, winning 43-31. Even the Twickenham crowd, which had been sympathetic to the All Blacks, began to appreciate that something extraordinary was occurring, as gradually it changed sides and started to support France. It must have been something quite unprecedented for a Twickenham crowd to support a French side, but it was true. There were tries simply to dream about from Lamaison, Dominici, Dourthe and Bernat-Salles. The poor All Blacks froze and it was painful to watch a truly great side capitulate in this manner. But that's probably why we play and support rugby. The generous Twickenham spectators rose to applaud the gallant French. It was a stunning victory. At last, there was something to cheer about in this dismal tournament.

The final in the new Millennium Stadium was a disgrace. The roof had been left open, even though it had rained for almost a week prior to the final and the pitch quickly became badly scarred doing a major disservice to the players. The closing ceremony lacked the panache of Ellis Park with its jumbo jets and President Mandela. The WRU had a difficult time of it. John O'Neill, the CEO of the ARU commented that the days are gone when you have a tournament the size of the World Cup run by part timers. The late distribution of tickets caused massive problems to overseas unions and RWC chairman, Leo Williams, had strong criticism of ITV's coverage. For the final, seats in the VIP area were duplicated and a number of very prominent guests had to move to other parts of the stadium. There were a number of very red Welsh faces.

The game itself was too much for the French, who tried too hard to find the élan that had secured their famous win against New Zealand. Once again, the Wallabies' defence was awesome and this, coupled with a steady stream of lineout ball, meant, in the end, that the Australians took the title for the second time, beating a tired France 35-12.

Yet again, the IRB's vision, strategy and structure let itself down. RWC1999 may have been a financial success, but as an exemplar for the new professional game it was a major disappointment.

*   *   *

With four World Cups under its belt, the IRB needs another major success and it is pinning its hopes on RWC2003 in Australia, where everyone is still soaking up the success of the Sydney 2000 Olympics. Since South Africa returned to the World Cup community in 1995, the quarter-finalists of every World Cup ought always to be France, England, Wales, Ireland and Scotland from the Northern hemisphere, and Australia, New Zealand and South Africa from the Southern. At RWC1995, Western Samoa (as happened in 1991) qualified ahead of Wales. At RWC1999, Ireland was the surprise failure, losing to Argentina, otherwise the quarter-finalists were the usual suspects, with Wales back in the fold.

For the first time since its inception, there is a very strong chance that all the old rugby-playing countries will qualify for the quarter-finals. Thankfully, sport is never a given and maybe RWC2003 will see the arrival of Argentina, Italy, Tonga or Samoa as a permanent threat to the old hegemony.

GLITTERING PRIZE...
OR POISONED
CHALICE?

Australia could turn out to be the perfect tournament
and, like RWC1995, one country will host it.
Sandwiched between the Melbourne Olympics (1956)
and the Sydney Olympics (2000), Australia hosted two
Commonwealth Games in Perth (1964) and Brisbane
(1988) and, of course, co-hosted RWC1987. Australia
regularly hosts the best – cricket and rugby league
World Cups, and Formula One, first in Adelaide, and
now in Melbourne. This wonderful city also hosts the
start of the Grand Slams in tennis.

What this means is that if you couple this wealth of
experience in hosting world-class events with the
fantastic weather expected for October and November,
along with the beer, the beaches and the barbies,

RWC2003 should be the best ever. Given that the IRB, especially Vernon Pugh, was very active in tipping the scales in favour of Wales, and not Australia, late in the day before the critical vote for RWC1999, some retrospective justice has been meted out.

RWC2003 reverted to four Pools but kept the number of teams to 20, with each Pool having five teams. This meant that the IRB had accepted the heavy criticism of the 1999 tournament whereby England, Scotland and Argentina had to play a pre-qualifier to win through to the quarter-finals. Unfortunately, keeping 20 teams only increases the number of heavy defeats by the professional countries against their amateur brethren. This is no longer acceptable and could lead to an increase in serious injuries. It will take such an injury settled in court before the IRB accepts its legal and moral obligations.

There are a host of innovations including five Pool games and two quarter-finals being played in Melbourne under a closed roof. There will be compensation payments for teams: A$430,000 for first-round losers, A$700,000 to quarter-finalists and A$850,000 for the four semi-finalists. Tied Pool matches at full-time will be classified as draws. Knock-out matches that are tied at full-time will have two ten-minute halves of extra time and a further ten minutes of sudden-death. If the RWC2003 Final is tied after all this, then a drop-goal competition involving ten players from each side comes into play (the equivalent of a penalty shoot-out) which sounds just a tad silly. If the teams still cannot be separated, there should be a replay.

But perhaps the most interesting innovation is that the Southern hemisphere point-scoring system has been introduced. Teams will receive four points for a win, two for a draw and none for a loss, and those scoring four tries or more, or those who lose narrowly by seven points or less, receive an additional bonus point.

Just as the Cricket World Cup in South Africa in February 2003 had problems with individual teams (especially India) and their sponsors, so it looks as though there will be similar issues that will have to have been put to bed by 31 July 2003. Players will have had to complete their contracts, agreeing to sign over their images and likenesses without any compensation. Intellectual property rights was an issue in 2003 and the International Rugby Players' Association will no doubt make sure that for RWC2007 it is a stakeholder in the contracts involving these rights.

As interesting for RWC2003 was the announcement that national teams would not be allowed to wear their own sponsors' logos on training and travel kit. England have O_2 and Australia have Vodafone as sponsors, but the main mobile phone company for the World Cup is Telstra. Ambush marketing is part and parcel of the whole industry and this unilateral action by the IRB will rebound in its face.

RWC1991 was the first time advertisers and media companies really became heavily involved in its promotion. This wasn't because of any love for rugby, it was purely the opportunities a white, middle-class game gave them. It was that good old friend, exploitation.

Until 1991, most of these companies had only had the IOC or FIFA accounts to work on. True, the IAAF had introduced a world competition outside the Olympics in 1983, but it has always struggled with its television and advertising audiences as Edmonton demonstrated in 2001. Athletics is still best when it is part of the Olympics or the Commonwealth Games, as Manchester showed in 2002.

The second World Cup's best (or worst) advert was for a New Zealand beer called Steinlager. 'Best' or 'worst' because it depended on whether you were a Kiwi or an Aussie. The strap line ran: 'What do you call an intelligent Australian? Answer: A New Zealander.'

In essence, this pop at the Aussies was probably a reaction to their well-worn joke about once going on a weekend visit to Wellington or Auckland only to find it shut. For much of the twentieth century, shops up and down New Zealand did not open on Saturday or Sunday.

It is true that there is an intense rivalry between Australia and New Zealand but, actually, when you look at the evidence, it is hard to understand how it has arisen. New countries, especially Empire or Commonwealth countries, inherited their language from their host nation(s), in this case England, Wales, Scotland and Ireland, but we all spoke English. With this language came powerful cultural landmarks – the Bible, Shakespeare, Robbie Burns, Dickens, Lawrence, James Joyce and Orwell, plus wider European influences from the music of a Verdi, a Beethoven or a Mozart. Sport is something that younger nations (after all, the nation state only dates from Cardinal Richelieu's work of the first decade of the seventeenth century) can adopt, mould and make their very own; it adds to the sense of nationhood. Sport has been the global language of the world since 1945, but this has somehow failed to catch the imagination of our major politicians. If only ...

In sporting contests between Australia and New Zealand, the Australians have been dominant – in rugby league, in cricket, in Olympic gold medals, even in a game called soccer (and even Poms are forgiven a little indignation as the Australians beat England 3-1 early in 2003 at the Upton Park ground of West Ham), but in rugby union, the All Blacks have generally asserted their dominance over their nearest neighbours.

Though the first unofficial British Lions (then Great Britain) tour in 1888 played games in Australia, the first British Lions tour to Australia and New Zealand was in 1930. The game was first only really played, appropriately, in New South Wales under the name of the Warratahs. Indeed, Australia's first international matches bore that name. In British Lions history, the great, great team of 1971 swept the All Blacks and its counties aside (P: 24, W: 22, D: 1, L: 1), although very little mention is made of the two so-called 'practice' games they played in Australia before setting foot in New Zealand. They lost one and won one.

But Australia remained a footnote in the history of the game; the reason was because the Aussies could not beat New Zealand at rugby union. The first game officially against Australia was in 1903 in Sydney with New Zealand winning 22-3. For the next six games, Australia won one in 1910. Eventually, Oz won at home in 1922 and then won their first game away in 1928 in Christchurch.

To date, New Zealand has won over double the number of games compared with Australia in the 116 played. But since Australia's wonderful Grand Slam achievement in 1984, the results have been 22 wins to New Zealand and 16 to Australia with one draw up to the 2002 season.

The Bledisloe Cup, introduced in 1931, was donated by Lord Bledisloe, Governor-General for New Zealand. The first game between the countries had been in 1903 so the series had been running for 28 years before the Cup became the symbol of supremacy. The Cup was played for as a one-off game ... but is now the best of three in a year. Gradually, Australia has put rugby union where rugby league and cricket has always been – ahead of the Kiwis. The laugh, of course, about the Steinlager advertisement in 1991 was that it was Australia, not New Zealand, who beat England at Twickenham in the Final.

Rugby union in Australia has had to struggle for recognition against Aussie Rules, played largely in the State of Victoria, and rugby league, which still dominates in New South Wales and Queensland. To do this, it added a third rugby State – ACT (Australian State Capital, now the ACT Brumbies) – to those of NSW and Queensland. This was an inspired decision. In the RWC winning side of 1991, the split of players was nine from NSW and six from Queensland, and in the cup-winning side of 1999, there were three from

New South Wales, eight from Queensland and four from ACT. With one of the lowest per head of populations playing rugby union (2.3 million worldwide) the Australian success has been truly remarkable and the ARU Committee, past and present, should take a deep bow, especially its coaching teams.

Although rugby has not been a featured event in recent times, it was an Olympics that caused a serious stir in Australian political society. Australian sport suffered a nervous breakdown of sorts at the Montreal Olympics in 1976 when it won one silver and four bronzes, but none in track and field. The result led ultimately to the creation of a National Sports Institute at Canberra, which then spawned a combination of Centres of Excellence and, eventually, individual sports academies for each of the major sports, and State-wide sports institutes. In developing these, Australia put itself on a par with what were then the models of sporting excellence from East Germany and the USSR, but thankfully they parted company over the issue of their performance-enhancing drug régimes.

Australian Rugby Union was able to benefit from the developments at Canberra and, while it would be foolish to lay every sporting success at its doors, what it gave the country was an unparalleled sporting focus. Its siting at Canberra may not have been obvious in 1978, given the duopoly of Sydney and Melbourne, but it did put it on the home plate of every politician. (Derek Wyatt first proposed a UK equivalent to the then Tory Sports Minister, Iain Sproat, in 1994. When the UK Sports Institute was eventually agreed in 1998, it was to be sited, not in London, but in Sheffield, a decision based on the power of two senior Sheffield-based Labour MPs, David Blunkett, then Secretary of State for Education and Skills, and Dick Caborn, then Minister of State at the DTI.)

Whatever ... sport is the new politics.

Given the current strength of Australian rugby, it's worth considering the current state of the All Blacks, and the NZRFU decision to give up hosting the Rugby World Cup in 2003. In doing so, the All Blacks management wrote the shortest suicide note in the history of their game. It beggars belief. You could argue, as we have, that the governing body of rugby union, the IRB, is a sandwich short of a picnic, but, by comparison, the Kiwis clearly couldn't even find the bread knife.

The All Blacks are now dining out at the Last Chance Saloon. It could take them years to recover and they would make an immense contribution to that process if they were to win RWC2003. They will now have to do this on the harder and faster surfaces in Australia against one of the strongest teams in the world playing at home as the defending champions. In some senses, if they don't win it may be that an unforgiving IRB would choose a joint bid from Australia-Japan-Fiji for RWC2019, assuming an African bid – say Namibia, Kenya or South Africa – was successful for 2011. Much will depend on the African Soccer Nations Committee decision on where they want the FIFA World Cup to be held in 2010. South Africa is on that list. It is doubtful whether the Rainbow Nation could afford two world-class events within the space of a year.

The All Blacks' *annus horribilus* began in 2002 when they thought they could persuade the IRB to modify its commercial contracts in favour of the host stadiums in New Zealand. In other words, although they knew when they signed with the IRB that it was the usual case of 'clean' stadiums for the IRB's sponsors (over and above the local Kiwi sponsors), they started a debate they must have known they were going to lose. For 'All Blacks', read 'All Over'.

Yet, curiously, just as Australia has found a way to make sport its religion, New Zealand was boxing well above its weight in diplomatic circles. Don McKinnon is Secretary General of the Commonwealth; John Hood, currently Vice Chancellor at Auckland University is to be the new Vice Chancellor at Oxford University and Dame Judith Mayhew, the new Provost at Kings College, Cambridge from October 2003. Given that New Zealand is not seeking to double its population and that its politics is more village hall than Albert Hall, you just might have thought that its own rugby union body would have touched base with its senior diplomats. But, just as in 1985 when it took the gallant Paddy Finnigan and Phillip Recordon to stop them playing in South Africa (a rebel tour went, nonetheless), so again in 2002 the NZRFU fell so unnecessarily on its sword.

Sport will be the new politics in New Zealand only when the two entities start singing from the same hymn sheet.

The world rankings moved around in 2003 because the Northern hemisphere countries had finished their season at the end of March 2003. However, the major countries then met in June, July, August and September in a series of warm-up matches, which included:

Australia v Ireland 45-16
South Africa v Scotland 29-25
Australia v Wales 30-10
South Africa v Scotland 28-19
Tonga v Ireland 19-40
New Zealand v England 13-15
Argentina v France 10-6
Samoa v Ireland 14-40
New Zealand v Wales 53-3
Australia v England 14-25
Argentina v France 33-22
New Zealand v France 31-23
South Africa v Argentina 26-25

The Tri-Nations fixtures were played in July and the beginning of August with each country playing on a home and away basis. The Northern hemisphere countries then played their last fixtures before the World Cup as follows:

23 August 2003 Wales v England
23 August 2003 Scotland v Italy
30 August 2003 France v England
30 August 2003 Ireland v Italy
6 September 2003 England v France

GLITTERING PRIZE ... OR POISONED CHALICE?

As a consequence, though England were ranked 1 in March 2003, to be honest there's hardly a cigarette paper of difference between the first four and our rankings would be:

1. New Zealand	11. Fiji
2. England	12. Italy
3. Australia	13. Tonga
4. France	14. Canada
5. Ireland	15. Romania
6. South Africa	16. Georgia
7. Scotland	17. Japan
8. Argentina	18. Uruguay
9. Samoa	19. USA
10. Wales	20. Namibia

Pool A throws Australia, Argentina, Ireland, Romania and Namibia together; Pool B has France, Fiji, Scotland, Japan and the USA; Pool C comprises South Africa, Uruguay, Georgia, England and Samoa; and Pool D will see New Zealand, Italy, Wales, Canada and Tonga vying for supremacy.

The only newcomer to the Rugby World Cup is Georgia. (Interestingly, it was in Tbilisi, Georgia, that the last rugby tournament of the Communist days took place between Romania, then a serious contender to world status, Poland, Czechoslovakia, the USSR and the Penguins, representing England, in August 1977. The Penguins beat USSR in the final.)

The quarter-finals will involve the winner of Pool D (our

predictions are in brackets, in this case, NZ) v the runner-up from Pool C (SA) in Melbourne; the winner of Pool A (Oz) will play the runner-up of Pool B (Scot) in Brisbane; the winners of both matches will go through to play one another for a place in the final, so it looks as if it could be a NZ v Oz semi-final in Sydney on 15 November 2003.

The winner of Pool B (Fr) will play the runner-up of Pool A (Ire) in Melbourne; and the winner of Pool C (Eng) will play the runner-up of Pool D (Wa) in Brisbane.

So the likely semi-final pairing here would be France v England in Sydney on 16 November 2003. Once again, the draw has ensured a Southern v Northern hemisphere final again in Sydney on 22 November 2003. And it would be a brave man or woman to bet against Australia not winning RWC2003 in its own backyard. Consider the evidence – in 1987, the major host nation, New Zealand, beat France; in 2001, the major host nation, England, lost to Australia in the Final; in 1995, the host nation, South Africa, beat the favourites, New Zealand, in the Final; and in 1999, one of the lesser host nations, France, lost to Australia. So, Australia has won two of the four World Cups by playing away ... now they have a chance to win it at home.

RWC2003 will be the third-largest sporting event after the Olympics and the Soccer World Cup. It will be followed on radio, on television and on the Internet at www.rwc2003.com.au. A global audience of 2 billion is expected for the Final. Australia's tourism industry will reap not just an amazing windfall through the generosity of the Kiwis, but it will be able to build on the image of Sydney Harbour Bridge we all saw at the dawn of the third millennium and the Sydney Games, for at least another five to ten years. Billions of Aussie dollars will flow into its Treasury. No wonder the new Aussie anthem is 'God Bless New Zealand'.

Of the other favourites for the tournament, England was ranked first for much of the 2002/03 season and has won its first Northern Grand Slam, against the three Southern hemisphere countries and the Six Nations. But ranking is ranking and World Cups depend so much on finding form as the Championship develops. France always does better than expected in a World Cup – the amazing underwater display in Durban, when France so nearly beat South Africa, will live long on the memory. New Zealand can never be underestimated and often starts at an amazing gallop, scoring huge points, but then starts to freeze at the semi-final and final stage. Ireland would be everyone's outside bet and, although South Africa seemed to have lost the plot earlier in the year, they have an uncanny knack of peaking during World Cups. They won it at their first attempt in 1995 and were third in 1999, so they cannot be ruled out. England and South Africa share Pool C in Perth, and whoever wins that game will proceed more easily to the semi-finals.

It would be wonderful for the game if the soccer equivalent of a Cameroon or cricket's equivalent of a Kenya made an appearance in the semi-finals. The game pines for a revitalised Fiji, Western Samoa, Canada, USA, Argentina, Italy or Japan to mount a credible challenge, but it seems unlikely. Australia versus England in the final (the best two sides from the Southern and Northern hemispheres) would be the choice of most pundits. Fortunately, we are frequently wrong ... nothing is a given in sport. But there is a danger in world rugby if the format is not rethought that the same old rugby-playing nations – France, England, New Zealand, Australia and South Africa – continue to dominate.

The RWC tournament manual for the 2003 Rugby World Cup weighed in at 111 pages. The thorny issue of players' image rights is the new battleground of this World Cup. Perhaps this is because, in soccer, Manchester United paid David Beckham up to £20 million as part of his overall contract for such rights. Agents are aware of the need both to protect their clients, as much as to exploit their true worth.

The difficulty for the IRB is that it has to pitch its 'rights' and 'sponsorship' packages at countries as diverse as Australia and Georgia. The ARU will pick up a quite considerable tab including business air travel for 30 players, and 12 managers/coaches/support staff; all accommodation costs at four- and five-star hotels; £45 a day per diem; and £7 laundry.

Nevertheless, most of the major Northern and Southern hemisphere countries will top this up to the tune of an additional £1 million with extra staff and extra bonuses.

*   *   *

France will host RWC2007 ... in theory. In fact, it will be shared once again with Wales, Ireland and Scotland, but not Italy. England ruled itself out because England dared to think outside the box and, once again, the IRB tinkered with the voting process

The RFU took a brilliantly innovative approach to the hosting of RWC 2007. They had originally put forward a radical new format which included two World Cups – one for the senior 16 nations and one for the next 20 qualifying countries. The latter was to be called the Rugby World Nations Cup, to take place in eight regions of England, the winner of which would automatically be promoted to RWC2011. Other initiatives included:

- Instead of the quarter-final contest following automatically from the first-round matches, the RFU proposed a 'Super 8' mini tournament in which the top two teams from the four Pools created two new Pools and four more matches
- Moving the tournament from the autumn to the summer

The most interesting part of England's bid was its financial assumptions, which would have grossed the IRB £140 million. In their submission, the French thought they could make around £100 million. We shall see. Essentially, England lost out because it was reluctant to allow matches in Cardiff, Edinburgh, Paris and Dublin. Extraordinarily, the IRB has consistently argued for rugby World Cups to be held in one country. Until there are fundamental changes to the structure of the IRB it will always remain a parochial rather than a global body.

The RFU had an excellent bid, which even the French acknowledged, so why did they suffer such an ignominious defeat? Keith Barwell, of Northampton, never a shrinking violet, provided the anwer: '... because they are perceived as arrogant and always right. They have no empathy for views that oppose their own.'

The bid cost the RFU a lot of money. A roadshow literally went round the world. They were received politely by other countries but the RFU officials did not come over too well.

The other Home Unions were quick to praise France. David Moffett, the CEO of the WRU said, 'The French Rugby Union are to be commended for completely honouring the deal we struck with them as host union in 1999 ...' The projections being made in the French bid for 2007 look likely to net the WRU a near £7 million return.

Bill Nolan of Scotland, declared, 'Having some Scotland Pool matches at Murrayfield is great news for the Scottish supporters from both clubs and schools across the country.' Well, they will hopefully offer more support than they did in 1999.

Ireland praised the work of Syd Millar and Noel Murphy as if they were part of the French team.

When France and England submitted their original bids, they included no matches outside their own country. Both were invited to resubmit their bids with, no doubt the message being, with a nod and a wink, to think about including other nations (i.e. the Celts) in the revised bids. The French took the nod and, hey presto, they got the full Celtic vote so they only needed three more votes. England might have felt that they were going to get support from their Home Union colleagues, but they were either absurdly naïve or did not realise that the Celtic animosity against England which started in rugby in 1884 was still alive and kicking

The French bid was the more conventional, with a 20-team tournament. Bernard Lapasset, President of the FFR, reported that he had offered England, through Francis Baron, a deal to make a new format and turn it into a joint bid. This was allegedly turned down by Baron. But France won the right to run the 2007 tournament with the voting 18-3 in their favour, with only Canada voting with England. Syd Millar, the IRB Chairman, said, 'The Council was overwhelmingly of the view that the structure should remain as it is, namely a tournament comprising 20 teams playing in four Pools of five.'

The IRB outmanoeuvred the RFU and the consequences of this have still to be played out. Our guess is that England will again withdraw from the Six Nations television contract, which is due for renegotiation in 2005. This time they will not mind being suspended from the competition. In 2003, the two most watched games on BBC1 were Wales v England (6.2 million) and Ireland v England (5.8 million). The Six Nations would collapse without England's presence. It is an absurd contract that favours the countries with the smallest rugby-playing populations. The money is evenly distributed between the four Home Unions; there are then further deals for France and Italy.

The BBC paid £65m for the UK rights to the Six Nations covering the period 2003–2006. It would not surprise us if England joins the Southern hemisphere's Tri-Nation tournament or even replaces South Africa. The Tri-Nations television deal is owned by Murdoch and has two more years to go (it was a ten-year deal in 1995). If it became a four-country tournament based on home and away, the media rights would be worth double what Murdoch paid in 1995 – so expect a deal within the parameters of £750 million and £1 billion. England would then reach a home and away deal with France and rugby in Ireland, Wales and Scotland would go back to being amateur and on a par with the lesser nations. It must be in England's long-term plans to undermine, once and for all, the aspirations of Wales, Ireland and Scotland to dine at the top table. It happened in soccer back in the 1970s when the Home International series was finally ended. Who would bet against it?

We should not be overly surprised to learn that the bidding for RWC2007 was shrouded in controversy. After all, so was 1991, 1999 and 2003. The IRB's move from Bristol to Dublin was not just for tax purposes, as the IRB's accounts have been offshore since 1989/90; the main reason it moved was to take it out of the media spotlight. Most sporting bodies move to Switzerland (FIFA/IOC) or Monaco (IAAF), not just for tax purposes, though that is a consideration. The IOC pays no tax in Lausanne but, as important, is the fact that the auditing rules are, how can we put this, slightly more helpful to companies, trusts and charities than they are in EU countries. But Lausanne, like Dublin, is out of the global media loop. This is a huge blessing to its executives and non-executives.

The financial state of play of the major rugby-playing countries makes interesting reading against the backdrop of the decision by the IRB to award 2007 to France. In the financial year ending 2001, England had a turnover of £54.7m with profits of £7.3m; South Africa managed £22m with a slight profit of £200k; Australia was similar with £20.7m and a profit of £120k, whereas New Zealand had a turnover of £16.3m but incurred a loss of £3.1m. Contrast this with the WRU being £66m in debt and the Irish having to reduce their reserves from £22m to £8m since the game went professional in 1995. England, too, will face renewed problems as there are no internationals at Twickenham in the autumn of 2003 and the television income has dropped considerably for them now that it is sharing the income from the BBC contract with the other countries in the Six Nations championship.

*   *   *

The 2011 Rugby World Cup should be awarded to a southern African nation bid, involving South Africa and Namibia, but it would be dependent on the latter country qualifying or being given an exemption. New Zealand would be hoping against hope that it could retrieve its besmirched reputation and land it. But if the African football authorities award the soccer World Cup to South Africa in 2010, then it is more likely that a bid from New

Zealand involving Fiji, Tonga, Samoa and even Japan would be welcomed by the IRB. By this time, we have every confidence that the concept of two World Cups, which was the thinking behind England's bid for RWC2007, will magically have been accepted by a newly reconstituted and enlarged IRB.

Rian Oberhauser, CEO of SARFU, has already confirmed that his country will be putting forward a bid for 2011. On 17 April 2003, he said, 'I will be surprised if England don't try a bid for 2011, but we will have to wait and see what they do. It is a bit soon to have a draft plan in place but we will now start talking about it, especially if the bids have to be in by 2005. We have already started talking to the Government about this. We met with them a few weeks ago and informed them of our intention to bid for 2011, and they indicated that they will support us.'

9

ONE GLOBAL GAME

Derek Wyatt was asked by his colleague, David Hinchliffe, the MP for Wakefield Trinity, to write a chapter in his book entitled A Westminster XIII during 2002. They became friends when Wyatt supported Hinchliffe and Peter Hain, MP for Neath, in their battle to have the former Welsh prop and St Helens front-row player Stuart Evans reinstated in 1994.

At the time, Stuart was playing in Union in France and was being paid to play. Stuart's crime was that he played rugby union and rugby league after the age of 18. He could not believe that he would receive a letter from the WRU banning him and, although the rules have changed, he is still bitter about the whole episode.

A committed socialist, David felt that rugby union as he

had experienced it was riddled with an anti-working-class ethos. There was (and is) only one game for him and that is rugby league because its clubs are steeped in their communities, much as the Welsh rugby union clubs used to be. In the chapter, Derek suggested that, by 2007, there should be one rugby organisation (League and Union) and one World Cup, but four competitions – major countries, rugby union; major countries, rugby league; minor countries (amateur), rugby union; and minor countries (amateur), rugby league. He always was a dreamer.

In the middle of the 1990s, it was fashionable to read pieces in the quality English broadsheets that the two codes of rugby were bound to merge. This was in part because of the sheer power that the Murdoch organisation had exerted on the game of rugby league. In 1994 and 1995, BSkyB (or Sky as it is better known) TV, the pay-per-view satellite broadcaster in the UK, persuaded a staid rugby league management team in England to move its whole calendar from an August–May schedule to a March–October one! Of course, there was a substantial financial inducement per club at a time when League was – if not broke – at least on the breadline. There were also noises off about alleged payments or success fees to some of the League's executive members to ensure that the clubs took the bait.

After a series of public rows within the game and within each club, the Murdoch–Chisholm (him again) axis was successful and, in the season 1995/6, the game moved en bloc. Today, most supporters now accept that this has not only saved the game but has also dramatically improved the playing standards. Just as important, crowds are up.

However, if the English game of rugby league was undermined and then under threat, it was nothing to the bloody war that broke out in Australia. It was no more than the usual feud between the Packers in the blue corner, owners of the Australian Rugby League (ARL), and, you've guessed it, the Murdochs in the red corner, owners of nothing much but just about to put a Scud missile into the game.

One of the many consequences of rugby union going open in 1995 was that the dividing line between its one-time rival rugby league became blurred. Hence the view that the games would merge within four or five years. Well, we were all wrong about that! True, players did cross the floor and, at one stage, there was a very real concern that English rugby union clubs were attracting the best rugby league players – Robinson from Wigan, Paul from Bradford. The underlying worry was that the long-standing League colts side would be trawled by their Union brothers. David Hinchliffe and Derek Wyatt sought a code of practice for this state of affairs when they jointly met with Dick Caborn MP, the Minister for Sport, towards the back end of 2001. In reality, though, what happened gradually was that the old rugby union players who had gone to League returned to Union – Scott Quinnell, Jonathan Davies, Martin Offiah, Scott Gibbs, Alan Bateman – by way of deals with either a club and/or their national squad. No international union player has gone 'North' since the game became professional. In Australia, Union has been able to secure the services of some of the great League players – players going 'South' – like Wendell Sailor, the effervescent wing three-quarter, and Matt Rogers.

There were, as you would expect, a number of experimental games. Wigan thrashed Bath under League rules 82-6 at Maine Road on 8 May 1996, but Bath won the return Union game at Twickenham 44-19 on 25 May. Wigan entered the Middlesex Sevens and won it easily in 1996, beating Wasps in the final 38-15. More recently, Sale played St Helens on 27 January at Knowsley Road. The first half was under Union laws with Sale scoring 41 points without reply. The second half, under League rules, was won by St Helens 39-0.

If anything, the codes have now settled into a more peaceful co-existence, especially as salary caps have been introduced in both codes in England, though as there is no rugby or sporting watchdog – an 'Ofrug' or 'Ofsport' – premier Union sides have been able to outwit their masters by any number of clever financial devices, including offshore pension funds. Wasn't it ever thus?

As both games move forward, their executives have to ask themselves this question: do they own themselves or are they at the mercy of the global media players? We have seen how a rather naïve Southern hemisphere rugby union world embraced a ten-year deal for a Tri-Nations competition. No doubt they would argue that Murdoch's deal was the only one on the table and that, if they wanted to pay their players (there is no strong club affinity) and keep ahead of the more conservative Northern hemisphere countries, they had to take what was on offer. Five years with a five-year renewable option would have been a better bet.

In the Northern hemisphere, the countries have not moved forward at the same space. From 1995 to 2000, England and France set about trying to gain admittance to the élite; Wales and Scotland went further and further backwards and Ireland did its best not to follow suit, although it was a close call. Between 2000 and 2003, England and France joined the élite, though France is, as ever, inconsistent, but on their day their flair and mental toughness is a match for all. Ireland now occupies the middle ground and has a chance to make it. Scotland and Wales look spent forces.

Against the élite – New Zealand, Australia, South Africa, England and France – since 1995, Wales has lost 80 per cent of their games (P: 36, W: 6, L: 30); Scotland likewise has struggled despite a first win against the Springboks in 2003 (P: 34, W: 5, L: 29) and Ireland has not fared much better (P: 33, W: 5, L: 28). The grand total for the three Celtic nations makes dismal reading – P: 103, W: 16, L: 87. In the British Lions tours of 1999 to South Africa and 2001 to Australia, the make-up of players from Wales, Scotland and Ireland was 18, eight and ten respectively out of a total of 72. The number of Welsh players playing for English and French sides shows a steady decline and will decline even further with the start of the new regional tournament, although some players who have finished their international careers could be tempted by France because there is no salary cap. Scotland still has a number of players plying their trade in England, headed by the Scottish captain, Bryan Redpath. Ireland has managed to bring back its players largely from England and, at the same time, to revitalise its provincial sides. The growing importance of the Heineken European Championships (inaugurated in 1995/96) has seen Irish provincial sides reach the finals in 1999, 2000 and 2002. Munster lost to Northampton in 2000 9-8 and to Leicester in 2002 15-9, but Ulster beat Colombiers 21-6 in 1999.

Against these developments must be placed the substantial, even volcanic, changes that have taken place off the field in the business world of sports management and sports sponsorship. ISL, once the darling of the international sports marketing world went into receivership in 2001 with massive debts. This took some believing. ISL was the idea of Horst Dassler, the son of Adi Dassler, the founder of Adidas and former maker of boots for Hitler's army. Horst joined Adidas in 1959, took over as Co-Managing Director in 1978 upon the death of his father and became sole Managing Director in 1985. After Horst's untimely death in 1987 at 51, the shareholding was split between his four sisters and Dentsu (Japan), the largest advertising agency then in the world (90 per cent of its trading, though, was in the internal Japanese market) with the Dassler family Trust holding the votes and a slim majority of shares.

Throughout the 1970s, Dassler had a vice-like grip on the rugby union market in England. It hadn't been difficult. He had used that old favourite, 'boot' money, either to provide Adidas kit free to the top 30 players in England (Derek Wyatt was one such recipient), or to pay the key players for wearing their kit in internationals. It wasn't difficult to organise; Adidas employed current rugby players like Robin Money from Leicester and David Ling from Ipswich/Wasps/Bedford and then Sale. Prior to an international, the Adidas reps would book themselves into the same Richmond hotel as the England team.

Eventually, this story finally made the tabloids via the *News of the World* in the autumn of 1982. The RFU simply did not know what to do. Instead of asking each member of the squad to discuss the issue with a leading QC, knowing that their evidence would be confidential and then asking said QC to write his report without identifying any player, the RFU fudged it.

A cursory glance at many of the ghosted autobiographies in the 1980s of the top international Northern hemisphere players of the day like Gareth Edwards, Phil Bennett, Bill Beaumont, Peter Wheeler, Andy Irvine and JPR Williams will reveal references to them wanting to be allowed to be paid for speeches at dinners or other non-playing events, including their autobiographies. Indeed, Fran Cotton (he wrote his own book and delivered it to his publisher in longhand) and Bill Beaumont were then subsequently banned by the RFU for accepting their advances and newspaper serial rights payments. How the rugby world has changed! Cotton was ultimately forgiven and called back to manage the successful Lions tour to South Africa in 1987 and sits on the RFU's Management Board. Beaumont is one of the RFU's IRB reps. Both were supporters of Cliff Brittle.

The leading players in France have almost always received benefits either in kind or in cash. Their local political system enabled the town Mayor to build relationships with his rugby team. The Mayor's slate was responsible for ensuring players did not have to work too hard in the week. It was ever thus. Indeed, it has reappeared with a vengeance over the past three seasons. France is able to attract both players from the Home Unions and players from Argentina, Italy, New Zealand and Australia, and coaches like Nick Mallett from South Africa (although he did have an England trial in 1980).

In 1994, David Hinchliffe asked Derek Wyatt to help him prove that rugby union players were being paid. Wyatt explained that the Bristol offices of Customs & Excise had commissioned a series of aerial photographs of the crowds attending games at leading Welsh clubs. They suspected that thousands of pounds of VAT were missing in their annual accounts. Customs & Excise then had the photos blown up so they could do a head count; they then compared these numbers with the 'declared' numbers on the balance sheets.

Hinchliffe then raised the issue with Stephen Dorrell MP, then Chief Secretary of the Treasury, on the Order Paper in the House of Commons, asking the Chancellor of the Exchequer what effect the known earnings of rugby union players has on the private club status of rugby union clubs with regard to the payment of income tax.

Dorrell replied that the Inland Revenue had confirmed that earnings of rugby union players had no effect on the private club status of rugby union clubs with regard to the payment of income tax.

Hinchliffe then asked why the Inland Revenue has taken aerial photographs of crowds at certain rugby union grounds, to which Dorrell stated that the Inland Revenue had not taken any aerial photographs of crowds at any rugby union grounds.

Hinchliffe probed again, asking the Chancellor of the Exchequer how many rugby union clubs were paying employers' National Insurance contributions in respect of earnings or financial rewards received by players, and if payments of Income Tax and National Insurance contributions from earnings through playing rugby union were being received.

The reply came back that the Inland Revenue's Special Compliance Office had started investigations into rugby union clubs, and that it was not appropriate to comment further.

Hinchliffe then asked for a statement on the progress of the Inland Revenue's special investigations into the Welsh Rugby Union; what tax had been recovered; what future arrangements had been made; and what similar inquiries had been made in England?

Sir George Young responded that rugby clubs were entitled to the same degree of confidentiality as any other taxpayers, so it would not, therefore, be appropriate to comment any further.

Eventually, the story was confirmed. Meanwhile, both

the Customs & Excise and HM Inspector of Taxes had challenged each club and their leading players to come clean. All this was done in secret.

Between its founding and eventual demise, ISL set the standards for the way in which what were then international sporting events – the Olympics and the soccer World Cup – was sponsored. They established the golden rules. There were to be no competing sponsors. Sponsors were targeted that were global in aspiration, if not in reality, with Dentsu's Japanese clients given priority. An élite club was created of these mega-brands like Adidas (of course), Toyota (Dentsu), Kodak, Coca-Cola, Toshiba (Dentsu), Sony (Dentsu), IBM and Levi's – but there were to be no cigarette companies. Eventually, this system was adopted throughout the world. RWC2003's main sponsors are Coca-Cola, Heineken, Visa, Qantas/BA, Telstra and Bundaberg Rum. England's sponsors are O_2 and Nike. It's hardly rocket science.

This led those brands who had been unsuccessful or who had not been seen as global, or who were outside the exclusive club, to eventually respond with charges of 'raiding' or 'hijacking' these events, which eventually became known as 'guerilla marketing'. Adidas might sponsor the ball in the FIFA World Cup 2002, but Nike sponsored the shirts for Brazil; the Royal Bank of Scotland sponsored the Six Nations 2003 tournament, but Lloyds/TSB (a rival bank) sponsored the RFU's large screen at Twickenham, and so on.

ISL did not have the market to itself, but it was first

out of its particular block. Others built on the sports market differently. Mark McCormack's established International Management Group (IMG) eventually developed into two companies – it looked after golfers, Arnold Palmer being his first client, and then branched out to represent other golfers then tennis players, then television personalities and journalists, then opera singers and conductors and, finally, managing events like Wimbledon and raising capital for the new Wembley Stadium. Now they can represent almost anyone in the media.

Meanwhile, its other arm, TransWorld International (TWI), busied itself with owning/managing and filming rights to some of these tournaments; it also created tournaments at which many of its own clients would appear. Only when Paul Smith joined them from Academy (he'd previously been at ISL) in the late 1990s did it venture into soccer, starting with an enormously successful venture in China.

McCormack's untimely death in May 2003 has caused some to ponder the ongoing viability of his enterprises, because he was so intimately involved with them. For the moment, his sons hold the reins. IMG finally became involved in rugby union by buying out the contract the IRB had given to CPMA (Callan, Palmer & Morgan Associates) in 1998/9 for RWC1991, RWC1995 and RWC1999. The IRB signed a further contract with IMG for the 2003 World Cup, but the contract is up for grabs from 2007 onwards.

The Rugby World Cup is probably the only Crown Jewel

event that Michael Watt and his company CSI (now called Octagon CSI) has not yet owned. Watt is a naturalised Brit but originally hailed from New Zealand. He sold his company in 1998 to Interpublic, a global advertising company based in New York. At the time, Interpublic was also engaged in rivalling IMG, and so in a short spending spree also bought Advantage International and APA, renaming the sporting venture Octagon CSI. Michael Watt was its (non-executive) Chairman, retiring from the board at the end of June 2003. Watt had built a different business model. He put his own money up front, often large sums, for the domestic and overseas television rights for the likes of Premier League (First Division in the old days) soccer clubs, for the Five Nations tournament, for England's soccer team, for cricket and so on. Of the three, ISL, IMG and CSI, he has played the shrewdest hands and is widely admired and respected throughout the world. Not only has he made money for his clients and for himself, he has also put millions back into the game without any attendant publicity.

The four musketeers of the sporting business world have begat many others. When we typed in 'sports businesses' into the Google.com search engine, it brought up 25,302 entries! Of course, there are those who think they can do it themselves. As a consequence, more and more rugby Unions and teams have brought this advice 'in-house'. England has a team led by Paul Vaughan, formerly of Octagon and, when we knew him first, at Whitbread. Under Vaughan, sponsorship and marketing revenue has moved increasingly upward. The Welsh Rugby Union took on the building of its Millennium Stadium in-house. Its debts are such that the major shareholder, Barclays, could foreclose at some stage in 2003 or 2004, depending on whether its new CEO, David Moffett, can balance the books and debts in time.

Moffett is no stranger to rugby, having been CEO of NZRU and Australian Rugby League during the 1990s. The IRB now has a sponsorship and marketing department. You pays your money and you takes your choice. But, with professionalism on the field, it is now incumbent that the management off the field is as professional. This is clearly not yet the case.

And as a warning to the IRB, there are several significant examples among other world sporting bodies of the result of an increase in secrecy, questionable dealings and a lack of consideration for the sportsmen and women who are directly affected by their decision-making.

Sepp Blatter, the presidential Chief Executive of FIFA, the world soccer body, took great exception to the book by David Yallop called *They Stole the Game*, which was published in the UK in 1998. He issued a writ against the editions published in Switzerland and Holland. The case in Switzerland is unlikely to be heard. (There are some interesting comparisons with Blatter's attempts to secure a favourable judgment in Switzerland with those of the former President of the IOC, Juan Samaranch, who also issued a writ, only in Switzerland, against the authors Andrew Jennings and Vyv Simson for their book *Dishonoured Games: Corruption, Money & Greed at the*

Olympics, published in 1992. It purported to be an exposé of Samaranch's life, including his role in the Spanish fascist movement before 1939.)

Yallop's case was heard in Holland and the judge found in favour of Yallop. The IAAF's former President, Primo Nebiola, was named, before his death, in an Italian Mafia hit-list for alleged corruption and malpractice. Malcolm Speed, the CEO of the International Cricket Council, refused to release articles to Derek Wyatt's lawyer, Jonathan Haydn-Williams, on five separate occasions, during the fiasco over whether New Zealand would play in Kenya and England in Zimbabwe in the Cricket World Cup 2003.

Three world cups ago, the IRB quite legitimately took the decisions to register in the Isle of the Man and Holland to avoid tax and unnecessary legal restrictions. It is essential that the sport's world bodies adopt a greater degree of accountability to its constituent shareholders: the players, the coaches, the owners, the spectators, the sponsors, the media players and the viewers.

We hope the IRB will take the lead.

The way it conducted itself in RWC1991, in the award of the World Cup to Wales and not Australia for RWC1999, and to some extent, the prevarication over RWC2007, has not augured well. We also think that the IRB's executive body should move to one vote for each country. Currently, the old, white Empire countries – England, Wales, Scotland, Ireland, France, New Zealand, South Africa (though change is happening here) and Australia – have two votes. This smacks of an old boys' club, not a world body.

The IRB began a process in 1995 to align itself to the IOC. In 1997, it was awarded full membership status, the notion being that the IOC would like rugby union to become an Olympic sport. Vernon Pugh, the Chairman of the IRB, to the surprise of many, even attended the inauguration of the new President of the IOC, Jacques Rogge, in Moscow in 2001.

A radical review of the IRB's constitution by an outside body, such as the National Audit Office or its equivalent, would help build public confidence. This should ensure that the power blocks that built up in the IOC are not replicated at the IRB. One starting point must surely be that the Chairman should only serve two terms and with Pugh's death the IRB has the chance to make the necessary changes.

It is also imperative that the Court of Arbitration for Sport in Lausanne is asked to develop an Accountability function for the IRB and all other international sports. At the margins of the next G8 meeting in the United States during January 2004, the leading sports organisations need to meet with their political counterparts; likewise, at the World Economic Forum in Davos (held every year in late January) sport should become a tabled topic, and wouldn't it be good if it was also a subject at the next World Trade Organisation meeting in Lancun, Mexico in September 2003? It is foolish of GATT to think it really acts as an accounting or sounding board for sport. It talks to itself. In the new millennium, sport needs to seize the opportunity to be part of the global political process.

Rugby union is now a vital part of the Commonwealth

Games as Manchester showed in 2002, with New Zealand winning the gold. However, the IRB missed a trick when it changed its mind about the nature of the event within the Games themselves. The original intention was for Tens, so cleverly masterminded by the Malaysian RU, to be introduced. Instead, the goalposts were moved and the old game of Sevens substituted. This complicated the development of the world game. There is already a well-honed IRB World Sevens series. In the series that finished in June 2003 at Twickenham, the All Blacks pipped England to the championship, despite England winning that particular tournament.

England also won tournaments in Brisbane and Hong Kong, giving them their best ever place on the World Sevens circuit. It was a remarkable achievement, particularly for the coach, Joe Lydon, who had come across from rugby league to be part of the England coaching team, specifically running the Sevens. He had to contend with a different squad for each tournament but was able to blend together a group of players who will now be competing very hard with New Zealand, Fiji and South Africa in 2004 to win the title.

Our hunch is that the IRB wants Tens to be the new game for the 2012 Olympics, especially if London or Paris wins the rights to host them. We doubt whether Beijing will introduce any form of rugby in 2008. China may have been a destination for Premier League soccer teams for the past five years (following Paul Smith's imaginative and ground-breaking work for both IMG and the Chinese FA) which has already led to Li Tie playing at Everton and Sun Jihai at Manchester City. It's not all been one way; Paul Gascoigne is now seeing out his autumnal years at the Chinese Second Division side Gansu Tianma, much as George Best did with the San Jose Earthquakes back in the late 1970s. However, rugby union is yet to become established in China. It is largely restricted to Red Army teams, as the Penguins International RUFC found on its inaugural tour there in 2000. The pioneering Penguins were the first Northern hemisphere country to tour there, but they were pipped by a university side from Australia who visited Shanghai. At least the Penguins did not run the wrath of the local militia. They have been invited back in 2004.

In 2000, Naomi Klein wrote a bestselling book, published in 25 languages, entitled *No Brands: Taking Aim at the Brand Bully*. Its central thesis is against corporate activism and it is a thesis that the IRB might do well to consider. Unless the rugby brand is built globally and with greater transparency, we may well see a situation where the players, as they have done with tennis and, to some extent, golf, will take over the game and administer it in a fashion that is more to their liking.

The players have moved quickly since 1995 to organise themselves into a kind of trade union. There is now an International Rugby Players' Association. In May 2003, they accused RWC2003 organisers as being 'out of step with modern global trends'. Tony Dempsey, head of both the IRPA and the Australian Players' Association, said, 'The IRB and RWC Ltd want to have their cake and eat it, too. They want to impose employer-related obligations on the players, such as unlimited use of their images in perpetutity for commercial exploitation without financial rewards.'

The globalisation of brands, the globalisation of advertising agencies and the globalisation of broadcast channels, especially as Broadband develops, have gone almost hand in hand. We should not be overly surprised. Murdoch's purchase of US-based DirecTV in April 2003 gave him global control of three critical territories for the pay-per-view satellite entertainment platform market – USA, UK and possibly elsewhere in Europe (through BSkyB) and the Chinese markets in the Far East as well as India (through the roll-out of StarTV). In case you haven't spotted the importance of these continents, America's population is in the region of 320 million; China, 1.4 billion, with neighbouring territories amounting to 500 million; and India comes in at a cool 1.1 billion people. Even an enlarged EU of 25 countries only has a population of 453 million. When India played in the final of the Cricket World Cup 2003 against Australia in South Africa, over 300 million viewers watched them at home. These demographics can only be produced again and again by sport. True, a funeral like Princess Diana's or an event like September 11 deliver global audiences but they do not generate them in the same numbers and neither, of course, can they be timetabled. The question is now: who has the power – the IOC, the IAAF, FIFA or the IRB? Do they have the rights, or does the power reside with the agencies that have the brands? Or is it the brands themselves? Increasingly, it seems to us that the brands have it.

In some ways, the work of ISL in creating non-competing global brands to work to promote themselves and, of course, the Olympics, was more radical than it appears in retrospect. As sport moves forward, we suspect that brands will start to want to own rights with sporting organisations. We shouldn't be that surprised. In the world of the wireless across the USA in the 1920s, the makers of washing powders and soaps sponsored dramas, hence the endearing term we now call *Neighbours*, *Home and Away* and *Coronation Street* – they were, of course, the new 'soaps'.

Some media players like Disney and Murdoch have bought ice hockey and baseball teams in the USA; in the UK, Sky, NTL, Granada and Carlton have bought into Premier League teams (they can only own up to 9.9 per cent). Media ownership rules differ across the world, but we sense that Murdoch's purchase of DirecTV will cause the goalposts to shift again. Maybe an England or an Australian XV would sell a portion of its rights (however defined) if it meant that they were financially secure for the next ten years. Murdoch is a brand too, and the ownership of his channels is an extension of that brand, irrespective of the names they are called.

The IRB has to chart its way through these waters. It needs to do so with a modern professional leadership.

As a road map to going global, we would recommend that the IRB develops a permanent relationship with its counterparts in rugby league (the Rugby League

International Federation). In due course, we hope that this would lead to a joint world board. Underneath this global board, we would hope that there would be four international entities – professional rugby union, professional rugby league, amateur rugby union and amateur rugby league. It's now too late for RWC2007, but for the next tranche of World Cups, we look forward to the emergence of complementary professional and amateur World Cups in both codes.

It would also be very remiss of us not to mention the continuing growth of women's rugby union. It had an unofficial world festival in New Zealand in 1990 which the hosts won. Subsequently, it ran its own World Cups in 1991 and 1994 with the USA beating England 19-6, only for this result to be reversed three years later with England winning 38-23. The IRB then recognised the next two World Cups in 1998 and 2002. In the former, the All Blacks beat USA 44-12, and in the latter they beat England 19-9.

These tournaments have grown in stature and should now sit alongside the main RWC schedules and not be a separate function. We hope that France will take a lead and invite the women to play in 2007. In the Women's Rugby World Cup 1998, a total of 16 teams participated, including teams from Spain, Kazakhstan, Russia, Sweden and the Netherlands, as well as the more predictable rugby-playing countries. For WRWC2002, Spain hosted 16 teams with Samoa the newcomer. The England team was given a send-off by the Rt Hon Tessa Jowell MP, Secretary of State for Culture, Media and

Sport, but her presence didn't, unfortunately, have the desired effect on the results.

Of the other issues that require attention, we would suggest that the IRB appoints its own 'flying drugs squad', that can test 24/7/52 in and out of season at their discretion. The use of steroids, especially by forwards, will always be an issue in rugby, but the use of hash, cocaine and Ecstasy should not be ruled out either. Earlier this year, France's South African-born Test player, prop Pieter de Villiers, tested positive for both cocaine and Ecstasy, which normally carries a three-month ban.

As the world of rugby adjusts to professionalism, it has been interesting to note that three Northern hemisphere countries have followed the path of their Southern counterparts by replacing their club structure with a provincial team – Wales (from August 2003), Scotland and Ireland. Ireland has seen major improvements at national level, especially in the Six Nations championship, but they have a poor record at World Cups, so RWC2003 will be a test for them. Only England and France still have a vibrant, if not always profitable, professional base. And it has been these two countries that have dominated rugby in Europe since 1995. France has always played a more subtle political game than England as far as rugby is concerned.

We suspect that England has to make another of those agonising choices in the next year or so. As a result of the RFU's intentions to put the finishing touches to Twickenham and because of the sheer professionalism (at some cost) that emanates from the senior team downwards, it cannot be too long before England's future as a part of the Six Nations is re-examined. We believe that, like its soccer counterparts, who ultimately dropped out of the Home Championship matches at the end of the season, which caused its demise, that the nation may have to contemplate dropping out for one season in order to win back its own broadcast rights.

10

THE FINAL
WHISTLE

No rugby club bar is complete without a discussion or two about the current state of play of the game. It seems to us that, as a result of a severe case of prodding by the Southern hemisphere countries, the game is finally moving from international to global status. There are, however, a number of issues that simply won't go away. As far as the clubs are concerned the major issue is promotion and relegation.

American Football, Super 12 rugby in the Southern hemisphere, and the Six Nations Championship in Europe, all seem to function without it, but there is an influential group – namely the Premier League owners in England – voicing the opinion that promotion and relegation in a fledgling professional sport like rugby will hold back the game rather than accelerate its growth.

The strongest advocates of non-relegation have been rugby administrators and coaches such as Nigel Wray, Rob Andrew, Mark Evans and Conner O'Shea. All of these are deep thinkers about the game so it is unfair to dismiss them as having vested interests. Keith Barwell, the Northampton owner, said in August 2001, 'My rationale is that you simply can't expect Premier clubs to spend, say, £10 million on ground improvement, activate long-term community projects to attract support and build youth squads and academies, and then have it all ripped away because of one poor season.'

The issue became a hot topic in 2002 when Rotherham was denied promotion to the Premier League after running away with the National One title. They did not meet the criteria set down in a document agreed by the RFU, the Premier Division and National One clubs. To be specific, it was Rotherham's own ground which did not meet these criteria, so they sought a deal with their local Nationwide League soccer team, Rotherham FC. However, without primacy of tenure, they fell foul of the regulations and their application for promotion was rejected. The problem with the criteria then was that they would not have been met by several Premier clubs such as Saracens, Wasps and London Irish, but they had already been 'grandfathered' in and could not be kicked out.

The issue is this: does professional rugby have different obligations? The game has started to come to terms with the change and, in general, is making a good job of it. As far as

England is concerned, the national game has never been better prepared. The club scene is vibrant, with increased gates each season and more converts to the game. The youth academies are working, and we should see more English-qualified players coming through the system. But here's the rub. You cannot run with the bits you like and discard those you don't. The majority believes you have to take the whole package – and that means promotion and relegation.

Nigel Wray has experience in soccer. He was an investor in Nottingham Forest and speaks from the heart when he says promotion and relegation are the reasons why 95 per cent of football clubs are financially shot to pieces. The problem is that those who put up the money are in a minority. If they walk away, the supporters always feel there is another local tinker, tailor or candlestick maker who will rescue the club. This might happen in football but, as Bristol showed, and London Scottish and Richmond before them, there are not as many people so ready to part with the readies!

Maurice Lindsay was head honcho of rugby league in 1995, and is now helping Orrell move mountains to achieve Premiership status. He argued with Nigel Wray, suggesting that no one could deny players, owners and spectators the chance of living their dream. Back in 1995, Lindsay opposed the promotion of Keighley Cougars when the boot was on the other foot. Dave Whelan, the multi-millionaire sports retailer who owns JJB Sports, has become Orrell's patron. Orrell were one of the strongest English sides in the 20 years before the game went open. They could not find a benefactor and slipped down the pecking order so dramatically that they ended up in National Division 2 and were heading for oblivion.

Whelan took an interest, Maurice Lindsay from that great rugby league club Wigan became involved, and now they are one of the pretenders to a place on the top table. However, Whelan is making noises about pulling out if the ladder to the Premiership is taken away. Other clubs who are attempting to move from the lower divisions include Exeter, Plymouth Albion and even Penzance & Newlyn from the National League second division. They are backed by a former player, Dickie Evans, and they are looking enviously at the top table; it is going to be increasingly difficult for any of the major Premiership owners to sell the closed-shop concept.

In December 2002, Cecil Duckworth accused the premier clubs of conspiring to ring fence the Premier Division by paying off Rotherham to the tune of £60,000 each. He supplied additional information to the OFT inquiry already underway, at the request of Derek Wyatt. The RFU took the allegation seriously and appointed Anthony Arlidge QC to investigate. He took five months to go into detail on the allegations and at the end of May 2003 he concluded 'that there is insufficient evidence to conclude that any payment was in fact made and some positive evidence suggesting that no money was paid.' The inquiry has probably cost the RFU in the region of a six-figure sum and if one or two of the owners carry out their threat to sue the Rugby Union for defamation it could cost considerably more.

Damian Hopley is the founder and CEO of the Players

Rugby Association (PRA), which is the players' trade union – hardly the sort of job you would think would attract a Harrow- and Cambridge University-educated Theology graduate! Having worked unpaid for two years at the inception of the organisation, Damian is now one of the most powerful men in rugby, looking after the interests of the professional rugby players in England and sitting on the board of England Rugby.

Damian was a centre for Wasps and played for England (he would have had a hatful of caps but for a couple of contemporaries called Guscott and Carling). He was in the side that won the World Cup Sevens in 1993. Unfortunately his career was cut short by injury. He was less than impressed by the support that he was given to return to the game, and this, as much as anything else, made him aware of the vulnerability of rugby players in the brave new world of professional rugby.

Despite having started with no funding, the PRA now has an income in excess of £400,000 via TV revenue, sponsorship, player subscriptions, events and commercial partners. To that end, the PRA now provides its membership with an Educational Fund of £50,000 and a central insurance programme of £100,000. Add to this legal and financial advice to assist players both during and after their careers, and you get an understanding of the good work the PRA is doing for its membership.

Hopley has some very strong views on how the administration of rugby can be improved. He is not impressed by some aspects of the IRB which he feels can sometimes be overly secretive. In a multi-million-pound industry, he extols the virtues of transparency at all levels. He also believes that the arrogance that exists at the governing-body level in the sport is fuelled by the 'blazerati' thinking that rugby is a far bigger sport than it really is. Until this complacency is dispensed with, he feels that rugby will never fulfil its undoubted potential.

As a trade unionist, he is against salary caps but recognises their worth in bringing stability to a volatile industry. He is, however, optimistic about the future and envisages players having full voting representation on a streamlined IRB. He also foresees a collective-bargaining agreement between the clubs and the players modelled on the successful American and Australian systems with player earnings being linked to central revenues. He also extols the value of a global international season and pan-European season, which could bring about the advent of summer rugby, depending on the agreement and investment of the TV companies. Finally, he is confident that we will see a Northern hemisphere side winning the World Cup within the next five years! Well, he would be, wouldn't he.

Lots of people just do not believe that clubs are sticking to the salary caps and believe that there are a number of scams to undermine it. Although Premier Rugby spends £75,000 a year on regulating the salary cap, Howard Thomas, Premier Rugby's Chief Executive, believes, 'Irregularities are difficult to detect because you can only audit what is in the books,' which basically means that, even though there are serious questions about the information coming from the clubs, no one is yet in a position to search below the surface and so suspicions will continue. Payments for houses, money via sponsors' budgets or 'employment' for players in notional posts for businesses of rich owners are a few of the ways that clubs seem to get around the salary cap.

Paul Ackford, in an article in the *Sunday Telegraph* in September 2002, illustrated the point by deducing that, if the 507 players registered to the 12 Premier clubs were paid the total sum of £22.25 million (£1.854 million salary cap x 12 clubs), then each player would receive an annual salary of around £44,000, including bonuses and other incentives. Accepting that this number of registered players includes players at all levels, with top players on at least £150,000 and the 'lesser' stars earning £100,000, the sums do not add up unless some players are playing for nothing. With some clubs having over 40 players on their books, it is difficult to see how they can stick to the salary cap.

Maybe it is time for a UK Sports regulator.

*   *   *

We opened the book with an analysis of how four people hijacked the game eight years ago. And the game at every level is still reeling from that statement in Paris in 1995 when the game went open. We doubt if there are four more people out there who will have such a profound effect on the game. But, as we try and second guess the fifth World Cup and assess its impact on the wider playing and watching public, we feel certain that by RWC2007 two changes will have occurred.

The first will be the power of the brands. Rugby union has a great brand but what happens if a Coca Cola or a Starbucks or a Fosters and a global media player joins forces and offers the best five countries a world cup of their own every year. Which board of directors or management committee will be strong enough to resist? It happened in a lesser way with Track & Field which was always the Blue Riband of the four-yearly Olympics, but which has to some extent spoiled its brand by having its own world championships every two years – a sure case of overkill. Brands need to be associated with success; brands need doors to open, brands need to play on. Who would have thought that HSBC, a largely risk-averse global bank, would pour £30 million or so per annum into Formula 1 motor racing? What does a risk-averse brand have in common with a sport where, albeit through nobody's fault, drivers die? What association, what link is there between the global bank, its customers and Formula 1? We'd suggest not much, and we doubt if many new accounts have been opened at the domestic level. But what Jackie Stewart sold HSBC was the fact that Formula 1 was the number one must-have global sport with spectators in their hundreds of thousands and a viewing audience every week or so of a couple of billion. And it was cheap. But it wasn't even that – what attracted HSBC was that when the circus came into town, they found themselves the guest of the president or the royal family or both. Doors opened that not even HSBC could have imagined.

So although we cavilled at the role of sponsors and the way that television in RWC1991 insisted that half-time was long enough for a three-minute ad break (or two), and though we looked down our noses at the £300 lunch before a game in a sponsored marquee, the fact is that busy people do business around sport. It's here to stay and if anything it will be developed to a higher plane over this next decade.

Players are brands too, as Nike knows only too well. They spotted Tiger Woods when he was eight years old and ensured his parents were well looked after until their son was old enough to sign deals with Nike, or understand the pulling power of IMG (his agents), or both. Nike pays Tiger $100 million but takes ten times that in golf sales. Not bad for a brand that until Tiger came along had no presence in golf.

To some extent a team game throws up fewer single brands, though David Beckham has shown how wrong our judgement can be. Eight years ago, Jonah Lomu could have been a global brand. Today, we suspect that the single individual that sums up rugby union and stands out from his contemporaries is the England fly half Jonny Wilkinson. We sense he is the Pele figure who will take rugby union global.

As brands coalesce, the mood music shifts. It shifts from the IRB to the players. In some ways we suspect that, over the next four years, the fight will be between the players and their agents and their respective Rugby Unions. The fight will be about rights: rights to sponsorship moneys, rights to intellectual property images, rights about Internet and broadband – and, just occasionally, rights about rights.

The smart Unions will quickly bring on board players giving them 30 per cent representation on all committees which will be ramped up to 50 per cent and more by RWC2007. The tough bit will be how players manage their time whilst allowing themselves adequate space to count all their money. For the next four years players' salaries off the field will double and treble. This will give them the chance to employ the best lawyers, the best accountants and the best agents. Smart Unions who cannot match this purchase power will be lost, maybe forever. These players will be the new Hollywood. We doubt whether too many Unions will understand the seismic shift towards player power. It happened at Wimbledon when the best players stayed away in 1972; golf is already a player's game; and track & field pays out huge appearance sums (£60k for a 100-metre runner). Rugby union is just around the corner.

If our analysis is right then the game simply isn't up to it. We have structures in place that will need to be constantly upgraded. Do we have enough managers, executives, administrators and thinkers in the game of sufficient calibre to cope? We know we do not. We expect the players will begin to want to take on the IRB. Hold on – it's going to be a bumpy ride.

If the game is to survive, the IRB has to be completely overhauled or go to the knacker's yard. Without a revolution within the organisation it will be eclipsed by the players' union. If a strong executive is not maintained at the IRB, the game will flounder. This, just as the game of rugby union takes to the global stage, would be a terrible outcome. But it will happen.

We mentioned that two changes will be in the vanguard by RWC2007. The second will be that the broadcasters will want time-outs to be introduced. At first each coach will be allowed to call one time-out per half. This is understandable. A coach cannot communicate with his players up in the stands or on the touch-line. He will be persuaded or seduced to accept the new rule. Broadcasters will want it because it will provide them with a wonderful new ad break from which they can make even more money.

You see the brands have it, the brands have it.

The game in England is thriving; in France the clubs, who have no salary caps, are attracting a whole range of overseas players; and the Southern hemisphere has a vibrant Tri-Nations competition with no player defections to rugby league. In fact, the traffic is now the other way. South Africa has its problems on the field but no one can write off a nation that is so proud and is coming to terms with the new order within their own country on the global stage.

What is needed is for the IRB to realise that rugby will never be more than a minority sport on the world stage unless it does something radical to help those nations below the top nations in the Northern hemisphere and the big three in the south.

There are over 90 countries in the IRB membership

but the majority of them are minnows in every sense, playing members, administration and interest. However below the top nine or ten countries (which now include Argentina) there is potential that, if left untapped, will either wither or lie relatively dormant for many years to come.

The IRB needs a policy of what we call positive discrimination towards the emerging nations. Discriminate against the major countries by letting them fund their own game and use the World Cup money for these ten or so countries below the top ten. But also realise that this will be a ten-year programme, and if successful, by the World Cup of 2015 there might be at least 15 countries that could win the World Cup instead of just four or five. What a tournament that would make, and imagine what it would do to the global audience?

Rugby has a chance in the next decade to take itself on to a new level. If this happens in the new professional era, it will be a Rugby Revolution indeed!

BIBLIOGRAPHY

The Rugby War, Peter FitzSimons (Harper Collins)

John Eales – The Biography, Peter FitzSimons
   (ABC Books)

Midnight Rugby, Stephen Jones
   (Headline Book Publishing)

Path to Glory – Wallaby Power in the 1980s, Mark Ella
   and Terry Smith (ABC Enterprises)

Nick Farr-Jones – The Authorised Biography,
   Peter FitzSimons (Random House Australia)

Super League – The Inside Story, Mike Colman
   (Ironbark Pan Macmillan)

Champions in Conflict – The Bath Revolution,
   Dick Tugwell (Robson Books)

Gareth Edwards – The Autobiography, co-written with
   Peter Bills (Headline Book Publishing)

Good Morning President – Rugby from the Top,
   JV Smith (George Allen and Unwin)

The Complete Book of the Rugby World Cup 1999,
    Edited by Ian Robertson (Hodder and Stoughton)
Brian Moore – The Autobiography, co-written with
    Stephen Jones (Partridge Press)
Cliff Morgan – The Autobiography, co-written with
    Geoffrey Nicholson (Hodder and Stoughton)
International Rugby Yearbook 2002–2003, Mick Cleary
    and John Griffiths (Collins Willow)
The Official RFU Club Directory 1999–2000, Edited by
    Stephen McCormack (Queen Anne Press)
*RFU Commission: Open Rugby – The Right to
    Decide 1996*
Presentation to the RFU by Sky Sports 1996
*Lowry Report on Administrative Structure
    Changes 1997*
RFU Nationwide Consultation 1997
The Mayfair Agreement 1998
'Putting England First' 2001
*Shareholders Agreement between the Clubs
    and the RFU, July 2001*
History of the IRFB 1886–1960
*CSI assessment of TV Rights for Northern Hemisphere
    Rugby 1996*
RFU Strategic Plan 1998
Management and Marketing in Rugby Union Clubs,
    Jim Saker and Sarah Massey, Loughborough
    University Business School
A Rugby Compendium, compiled by John M. Jenkins
    (The British Library)
An Administrative Structure for the 21st Century,
    John Jeavons-Fellows
Mud, Blood and Money, Ian Malin
    (Mainstream Publishing)

APPENDIX A

Reproduced by kind permission of the RFU

Bone Wells Associates

Economic & Planning Consultants

RUGBY FOOTBALL UNION

**RUGBY WORLD CUP 2007
ECONOMIC IMPACT
ON THE UK**

REPORT

Omnibus Business Centre
39-41 North Road
London
N7 9DP
Tel: 020 7687 2020
Fax: 020 7687 2023

Rugby World Cup 2007 – Economic Impact on the UK

To estimate the economic impact in the UK of hosting the Rugby World Cup (RWC) in England in 2007, the approach is to estimate all spectators' consumption in the UK because of the tournament. This consumption occurs both on-site and off-site, i.e. in the stadiums in the way of tickets, car parking, food and drinks, to mention but a few, and outside the stadium such as transport, other sorts of entertainment, accommodation, retail, etc.

Consumption on-site has already been estimated in the previous report on the revenue estimate of the RWC. It has been computed as gross income to the Rugby Football Union (RFU) and other businesses, i.e. firms providing goods and services in-site.

Regarding consumption off-site, the starting point is the estimated attendance to the cup and the bowl referred to in the previous report. It is then necessary to calculate the actual number of visitors and their expenditure in the UK.

➢   Visitors' estimate

Attendances are not an accurate estimate of visitors, as some people would attend more than one game. According to the RWC held in Wales in 1999, people attended an average of one and a half games. A higher figure is more appropriate to this RWC as there will be two tournaments at the same time. It has been assumed that each spectator attends two and a half games on average.

Visitors are then divided according to their origin, i.e. those coming from England, other UK and from overseas. These proportions have been estimated based on visitor's origin in the RWC 1999 and by taking into account that more Europeans are expected to come as this RWC has two tournaments and also England is more accessible in terms of transport and distance. Consequently, 66% of spectators are assumed to come from England, 10% from the rest of the UK, and 24% from overseas.

Visitors will not all come alone, some will bring their families. It is assumed that 10% of visiting Europeans and 20% of longer distance origins come in family groups.

2

APPENDIX A

Having split spectators by origin, adjustments for displacement need to be made, to take into account only spectators and expenditure which is entirely additional. In the case of UK residents, most of them would spend money on transport, food and drinks, car parking, and on tickets to any other entertainment. Therefore, their expenditure is not due to the RWC, for there is limited effect on the UK economy from hosting the event. Only the expenditure coming from those UK residents who would otherwise have gone away on holidays or for any other purpose (for example spending instead of saving) is considered to occur because of the RWC. In the same way, some overseas spectators coming to the UK to attend the RWC would have come anyway. With respect to overseas visitors, two scenarios have been set up. A moderate one assuming that 20% of overseas would have come anyway, which is in line with a survey for the RWC held in Wales in 1999, and a conservative one where the proportion of overseas coming anyway is assumed to be 40%.

After accounting for displacement, the new 'distribution' of visitors is calculated as: England 19%, other UK 3% and overseas 78%. Thus, the great bulk of the total impact of the RWC in the UK economy comes from the expenditure of overseas visitors.

The following are the estimated number of visitors for the moderate scenario in the categories mentioned above:

- Attendance   1,827,086

- Visitors
England	482,351
Other UK	73,083
Overseas	175,400
Total	730,834

- Net visitors (after displacement)
England	33,765
Other UK	5,116
Overseas	140,320
Total	179,201

- Overseas coming with family   24,556

3

THE RUGBY REVOLUTION

➢ Expenditure estimate

Expenditure per person per day has been estimated according to expenditure in the RWC 1999 and to inbound tourists' daily expenditure in the UK. England residents are assumed not to pay for accommodation, instead when travelling to a game they come back on the same day or they stay with friends or family. Ticket prices and all on-site consumption have been excluded. Length of stay is different depending on origin of visitors, and the farther people are coming from, the more they are expected to stay.

The following tables show the expenditure per visitor origin (moderate scenario):

Origin	Length of stay	£ per person per day	Total £
England	4	30	4,051,745
Other UK	3	80	1,227,802
Overseas	14	100	162,069,811
Total			167,349,358
With additionality			158,876,606

Origin	Length of stay	£ per person per day	Total £
Europeans	10	210	7,366,810
Rest overseas	18	250	94,716,123
Total			102,082,933
With additionality			96,978,786

➢ Media expenditure

An estimate for journalists coming to the RWC and their expenditure has been based on the previous RWC, and subsequently grossing up those figures to account for two tournaments, that is a total of 98 games over a period of six weeks. Total media expenditure accounts for £ 1,380,000, and a total of 2,300 journalists for the two tournaments.

4

APPENDIX B

RWC FINANCES 1987–99

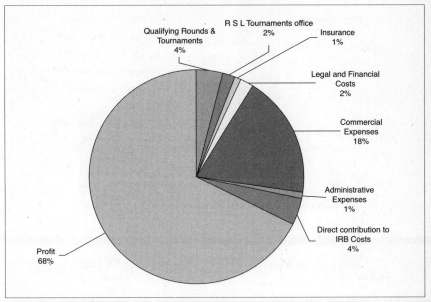

RWCL EXPENSES AS A PERCENTAGE OF INCOME (1999)

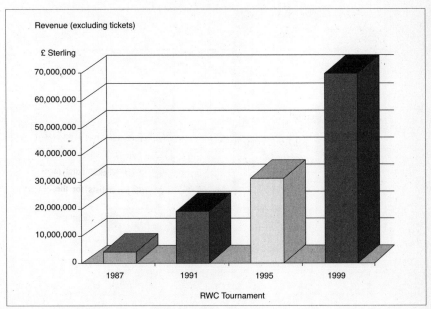

RWC: COMMERCIAL REVENUE GROWTH

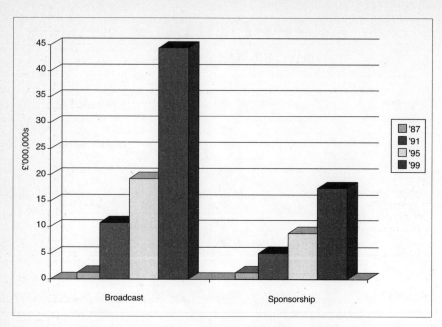

RWC: PRIMARY REVENUE BREAKDOWN

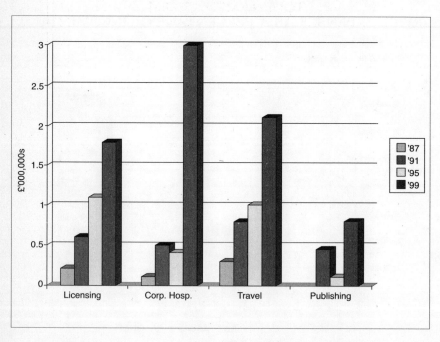

RWC: SECONDARY REVENUE BREAKDOWN

APPENDIX B

	Budget	Actual
	£M	£M
Commercial Income	70,500,000	68,748,178
Total Income	70,500,000	69,749,178
Qualifying Rounds & Tournaments	2,100,000	2,536,606
RSL Tournament office	1,100,000	1,429,834
Insurance	800,000	825,777
Legal and Financial Costs	2,500,000	1,699,050
Commercial Expenses	13,400,000	12,741,360
Administrative Expenses	1,700,000	1,000,234
Direct contribution to IRB Costs	2,500,000	2,500,000
Total Expenditure	24,100,000	22,732,861
Net Result	46,400,000	47,016,317

RWC: GRAND TOTAL COMMERCIAL AND TOURNAMENT (1999)

APPENDIX C

THE ALL-TIME RECORDS IN 5/6 NATIONS

INTERNATIONAL CHAMPIONSHIP WINNERS

SEASON	WINNERS
1882-83	ENGLAND
1883-84	ENGLAND
1884-85	NOT COMPLETED
1885-86	ENGLAND & SCOTLAND (shared)
1886-87	SCOTLAND
1887-88	NOT COMPLETED
1888-89	NOT COMPLETED
1889-90	ENGLAND & SCOTLAND (shared)
1890-91	SCOTLAND
1891-92	ENGLAND
1892-93	WALES
1893-94	IRELAND
1894-95	SCOTLAND
1895-96	IRELAND
1896-97	NOT COMPLETED
1897-98	NOT COMPLETED
1898-99	IRELAND
1899-1900	WALES
1900-01	SCOTLAND
1901-02	WALES
1902-03	SCOTLAND
1903-04	SCOTLAND
1904-05	WALES
1905-06	IRELAND & WALES (shared)
1906-07	SCOTLAND
1907-08	WALES
1908-09	WALES
1909-10	ENGLAND
1910-11	WALES
1911-12	ENGLAND & IRELAND (shared)
1912-13	ENGLAND
1913-14	ENGLAND
1914-15	NO COMPETITION
1915-16	NO COMPETITION
1916-17	NO COMPETITION
1917-18	NO COMPETITION
1918-19	NO COMPETITION
1919-20	ENGLAND, SCOTLAND & WALES (shared)
1920-21	ENGLAND
1921-22	WALES
1922-23	ENGLAND
1923-24	ENGLAND
1924-25	SCOTLAND
1925-26	SCOTLAND & IRELAND (shared)
1926-27	SCOTLAND & IRELAND (shared)
1927-28	ENGLAND
1928-29	SCOTLAND
1929-30	ENGLAND
1930-31	WALES

SEASON	WINNERS
1931-32	ENGLAND, WALES & IRELAND (shared)
1932-33	SCOTLAND
1933-34	ENGLAND
1934-35	IRELAND
1935-36	WALES
1936-37	ENGLAND
1937-38	SCOTLAND
1938-39	ENGLAND, WALES & IRELAND (shared)
1939-40	NO COMPETITION
1940-41	NO COMPETITION
1941-42	NO COMPETITION
1942-43	NO COMPETITION
1943-44	NO COMPETITION
1944-45	NO COMPETITION
1945-46	NO COMPETITION
1946-47	WALES & ENGLAND (shared)
1947-48	IRELAND
1948-49	IRELAND
1949-50	WALES
1950-51	IRELAND
1951-52	WALES
1952-53	ENGLAND
1953-54	ENGLAND, FRANCE & WALES (shared)
1954-55	WALES & FRANCE (shared)
1955-56	WALES
1956-57	ENGLAND
1957-58	ENGLAND
1958-59	FRANCE
1959-60	FRANCE & ENGLAND (shared)
1960-61	FRANCE
1961-62	FRANCE
1962-63	ENGLAND
1963-64	SCOTLAND & WALES (shared)
1964-65	WALES
1965-66	WALES
1966-67	FRANCE
1967-68	FRANCE
1968-69	WALES
1969-70	WALES & FRANCE (shared)
1970-71	WALES
1971-72	NOT COMPLETED
1972-73	QUINTUPLE TIE
1973-74	IRELAND
1974-75	WALES
1975-76	WALES
1976-77	FRANCE
1977-78	WALES
1978-79	WALES
1979-80	ENGLAND
1980-81	FRANCE

SEASON	WINNERS
1981-82	IRELAND
1982-83	FRANCE & IRELAND (shared)
1983-84	SCOTLAND
1984-85	IRELAND
1985-86	FRANCE & SCOTLAND (shared)
1986-87	FRANCE
1987-88	WALES & FRANCE (shared)
1988-89	FRANCE
1989-90	SCOTLAND
1990-91	ENGLAND
1991-92	ENGLAND
1992-93	FRANCE
1993-94	WALES*
1994-95	ENGLAND
1995-96	ENGLAND*
1996-97	FRANCE
1997-98	FRANCE
1998-99	SCOTLAND
1999-2000	ENGLAND
2000-2001	ENGLAND*
2001-2002	FRANCE
2002-2003	ENGLAND

*Indicates winners of Five/Six Nations Trophy (introduced 1993) on points difference.

England have won the title outright 25 times, Wales 22, Scotland 14, France 12, Ireland 10 and Italy 0.

INDEX